Organize Your Library!

ALA Neal-Schuman purchases fund advocacy, awareness, and accreditation programs for library professionals worldwide.

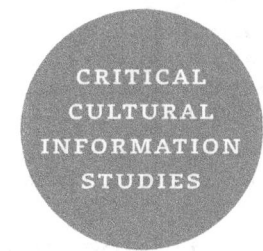

CRITICAL CULTURAL INFORMATION STUDIES

ORGANIZE YOUR LIBRARY!

Developing the Collective Power of Library Workers

Angelo Moreno, Kelly McElroy, Meredith Kahn, and Emily Drabinski

Chicago | 2025

Critical Cultural Information Studies is a book series to help advance the library field's discussions and understanding of often difficult issues, such as structural racism, equity, sexuality, disability, oppression, privilege, power, intersectionality, and inclusion and belonging.

Nicole A. Cooke is the series editor of Critical Cultural Information Studies. Cooke is the Augusta Baker Endowed Chair and associate professor at the School of Information Science at the University of South Carolina.

CCIS ADVISORY BOARD
Jeanie Austin, San Francisco Public Library
Mónica Colón-Aguirre, University of South Carolina
LaVerne Gray, Syracuse University
Sandra Hughes-Hassell, University of North Carolina
Robin Kurz, Dorchester County Library
Gerald Moore, Charleston County Public Library
Teresa Neely, University of New Mexico
Kellee E. Warren, University of Illinois at Chicago

© 2025 by Angelo Moreno, Kelly McElroy, Meredith Kahn, and Emily Drabinski

Extensive effort has gone into ensuring the reliability of the information in this book; however, the publisher makes no warranty, express or implied, with respect to the material contained herein.

ISBNs
979-8-89255-522-7 (paper)
979-8-89255-323-0 (pdf)

Library of Congress Cataloging-in-Publication Data
Names: Moreno, Angelo, 1983- author | McElroy, Kelly author | Kahn, Meredith, 1980- author | Drabinski, Emily author
Title: Organize your library! : developing the collective power of library workers / Angelo Moreno, Kelly McElroy, Meredith Kahn, and Emily Drabinski.
Description: Chicago : ALA Neal-Schuman, 2025. | Series: Critical cultural information studies | Includes bibliographical references and index.
Identifiers: LCCN 2025011828 (print) | LCCN 2025011829 (ebook) | ISBN 9798892555227 paperback | ISBN 9798892553230 pdf
Subjects: LCSH: Collective bargaining—Librarians—United States | Collective bargaining—Library employees—United States | Librarians' unions—United States | Library employees—Labor unions—United States
Classification: LCC Z682.35.C64 M67 2025 (print) | LCC Z682.35.C64 (ebook) | DDC 331.89/04102—dc23/eng/20250604
LC record available at https://lccn.loc.gov/2025011828
LC ebook record available at https://lccn.loc.gov/2025011829

Book design by Alejandra Diaz in the Leo, Brother 1816 and Laski Slab typefaces.

∞ This paper meets the requirements of ANSI/NISO Z39.48-1992 (Permanence of Paper).

Printed in the United States of America
29 28 27 26 25   5 4 3 2 1

Disclaimer: This work does not represent the views of the authors' employers. The authors and individuals quoted herein are speaking on their own behalf and not in any official capacity as representatives of their unions or their places of employment.

"This publication is designed to provide accurate and authoritative information in regard to the subject matter covered. It is sold with the understanding that the publisher is not engaged in rendering legal, accounting, or other professional service. If legal advice or other expert assistance is required, the services of a competent professional person should be sought" (from a Declaration of Principles adopted jointly by a Committee of the American Bar Association and a Committee of Publishers).

Contents

Foreword by Jane Slaughter *vii*
Acknowledgments *ix*
Introduction *xi*

1. **What Is a Union and Why Do I Need One?** 1
2. **How Do We Start?** 11
3. **Winning a Union** 27
4. **What Makes Library Workers Different?** 39
5. **Campaigns** 51
6. **Contracts** 63
7. **Dealing with the Boss** 83
8. **Our Vision for the Future** 95
9. **Bonus: If You're Reading This and You're the Boss** 99

References *107*
About the Authors *113*
Index *115*

Foreword

The American Library Association (ALA) is publishing this book at just the right time—when unions are on the rise. In 2023 union members in auto plants and on movie sets startled observers with their willingness to strike to win a fair share of corporate profits. Teachers in Portland, Oregon, and Los Angeles, California, won community support with their strikes for students' needs as well as their own. The year before, underpaid Starbucks and Amazon workers decided that a union was the only way to win some say over their working conditions.

In fact, that's true for just about any employee, no matter their salary or their education. On our own, we have little leverage. With a union, we have the power of numbers—and we can "get it in writing." That's security: knowing that your salary, your benefits, or your hours can't be changed by a fiat from above. Your working conditions are decided by a collectively negotiated agreement rather than by an individual's personal quirks.

It's exciting to see library workers joining the surge to join unions. Where I live in Detroit, the city's public library workers have been Auto Workers members (yes!) for decades. In 2023 the library workers in the small suburb of Ferndale formed their own union with the NewsGuild (part of the Communications Workers) and immediately reached out for public support. Residents and other allies jammed library board meetings to say their piece. Board members sat stone-faced as we urged them to recognize the union; they hired a union-busting lawyer instead. No matter; workers voted by 90 percent to form their union. During Pride Month in June, a local hate group removed all the books on the library's youth Pride displays. At the next board meeting, union supporters and LGBT residents demanded that management take action to protect workers from hate groups; they declined.

Foreword

In the fall, though, Ferndale union members ratified a contract with pay increases and annual raises, a cost-of-living bonus based on property valuations, more time off, paid lunches, and a labor-management committee that meets at least four times a year to discuss issues that arise.

This book will give you the arguments for why library workers need unions. Yes, a union contract can raise salaries substantially and codify the rules for overtime pay and time off. No, a contract won't limit library workers' autonomy—quite the opposite. A union contract can include the protections that library workers need in order to stand up to assaults on the freedom to read. What will help the Ferndale library workers, and many others, to resist book bans is that they are no longer at-will employees; their jobs are secure. What's more, their contract says that management must address harassment by patrons.

It's so much easier to join coalitions that are defending the First Amendment if you have an organization to do so!

Just as important, this book is how-to. It tells the stories of those who've started their own unions, negotiated contracts, and bargained for the common good of their communities.

Reading these stories helps others see that they can do it too.

Today is the best of times in that unions are on the ascendant—and welcoming every worker to join. It's the worst of times in that the very right to research and hold our own ideas is under fierce assault. Forming a union at your library lies at the intersection of these two vectors.

—JANE SLAUGHTER
Detroit, Michigan
December 2023

JANE SLAUGHTER is a former editor of *Labor Notes*, a member of the *Labor Notes* board, and coauthor of *Secrets of a Successful Organizer, Working Smart,* and *Concessions and How to Beat Them.* She is an enthusiastic library patron.

Acknowledgments

Thank you to the unionists who spoke with us about their work and organizing: Alan, Alexis, Allee, Althea, Alyssa, Amy, Andrea, Anita, Becca, Bonnie, Bridget, Chelsea, Chris, Christina, Crystal, Dave, Elissa, Emily, Ginny, Hélène, Jackie, Jade, Jane, John, Katie, Kendra, Kristen, Libby, Maria, Maty, Patricia, and Tara. Thank you for sharing your stories for this book, but most of all, thank you for all your work and struggle.

Labor researcher, author, and activist Jane McAlevey did not live to see this book as a finished product, but we are all grateful we had the opportunity to learn from her. Jane's work was an inspiration to all of us long before we came together to write this book, and her prodigious output will continue to inspire new generations of organizers in the years to come.

Thank you to Jane Slaughter and to the folks at *Labor Notes* for their practical guidance.

Thank you to Katie Dover-Taylor, Justin Joque, Jasmine Shumaker, and Jen Wilson for their close reading and thoughtful feedback, which helped strengthen our manuscript. Our sincere thanks to Rachel Chance and the folks at ALA Editions | ALA Neal-Schuman for helping us get this work out into the world.

Angelo would like to thank all of his coworkers at the East Lansing Public Library in Michigan who entertained the many times he asked them to stand up for themselves, together. They made the library better, and making the world a better place starts with the people we see every day at our jobs, in our neighborhoods, and in all the spaces in which we're thrown together with others by forces beyond our immediate control.

Emily would like to thank all the library workers across the country, big city and small, public, school, and academic, of every rank and status, who made time to share their experiences with her during her term as president of the American Library Association. Libraries work because we do!

Acknowledgments

Kelly would like to thank all her United Academics at Oregon State University (UAOSU) comrades for everything she has learned about unions, particularly Jan for helping her think through so many things out loud. Muchísimas gracias al Instituto de Investigaciones Bibliotecológicas y de la Información at the Universidad Autónoma de México, which hosted her during much of the writing of this book.

Meredith would like to thank the family, friends, colleagues, and fellow union members who still want to hang out with them even though they now treat everything like an organizing conversation.

Introduction

We are big fans of libraries. We think they are special, unique places that fulfill an important role in our society. We know that our work in libraries enriches people's lives. Those of us in public libraries know that the services we provide are particularly valuable and important to the most marginalized and under-resourced members of our communities. In school libraries, we add a crucial set of skills and support for children of all ages. In academic libraries, we know that our work enriches the intellectual lives of our students and helps them achieve their academic and career goals. We enjoy and take pride in our work. And yet, it is work (Ettarh, 2018). Like any job, it can be stressful, unfairly compensated, chaotic, oppressive, degrading, and sometimes even toxic. Library workers, noble that our profession may be, are not immune to the multitude of problems that face anyone who works for a boss in exchange for a wage. We believe that when library staff understand that they are workers and join the labor movement, they will be best equipped to shape the conditions at their library and beyond.

Our vision extends far beyond simply winning more library worker unions. We want to build collective power so that we can transform society. We want to develop the power of ordinary people to change the conditions of our lives. This bottom-up vision of power is different from views that position a small minority to speak and advocate for the rest of us, supposedly on our behalf. Because those top-down approaches "fail to involve ordinary people in any real way," they fail to build the power of the only force capable of truly bringing about the kinds of societal transformations we so desperately need (McAlevey, 2016, p. 9). At our libraries, we should be actively inviting our coworkers to meaningfully participate in shaping both the conditions under which they labor and the conditions that govern the library itself. We should be recruiting our fellow workers to meaningfully participate in setting the missions and goals of our libraries. We should be developing the capability of all library workers to build systems of justice and accountability at our libraries. Organized labor is uniquely positioned to serve as training grounds for building this type of collective power.

Community members will benefit from libraries staffed by empowered, unionized workers who embrace this broad vision of collective power. Marilyn Sneiderman and Stephen Lerner (2023), two longtime veterans of the labor movement, believe that unions should expand their goals beyond that of simply gaining new members. "[I]f our goal is just to gain new members and we do not ground our work in a broader movement for transformational change at every level of society," they write, "we will be successful neither in organizing significant numbers of new members nor in addressing critical issues of defending democracy, racial and economic inequality, and climate change that are central to workers and the future of our world" (p. 77). Libraries, especially public libraries, are often already directly serving working-class communities suffering the effects of racial and economic inequality, civic disempowerment, and climate change. McAlevey and Lawlor (2023) argue that "working conditions in the public sector essentially determine the quality and quantity of public services the working class receives as a whole" and that "strong unions ready to effectively win public-interest demands" can lead to stronger protections for "hard-won rights in the years between increasingly gerrymandered elections" (p. 11). Library workers, therefore, should expand what we are fighting for and include these communities in our theories and acts of collective power.

As individuals, many library bosses may hold racial and economic justice, democracy, and climate justice among their own personal values and aspirations. But the structures of our organizations make it difficult for people who climb to the top of the organizational pyramid to see clearly what's happening down at the base. Library bosses are often no longer working at service desks and may have little real understanding of the day-to-day lives of library patrons or the workers who directly interact with them. In the worst case, they are more interested in their own advancement and compensation than they are interested in aligning our institutions with the ongoing struggles for racial and economic justice, democracy, and climate justice. In the best case, the incentives that surround them and the options available to them exercise severe limitations on their political imagination. As union leader and historian Donna Murch (2022) cautions, "proximity to power rarely equals power" (p. 82). This is why we cannot rely on library bosses alone to bring about the kinds of transformations we need, both within and beyond our institutions.

About Us

This book was born at the crossroads of multiple organizing paths in libraries during and immediately following the COVID-19 pandemic. In the fall of 2022, Emily Drabinski brought all of us together to pitch the idea that we write a book about organizing in libraries, intended for our fellow library workers eager to build their collective power on the job. It took little convincing—in fact, we wrote our entire book proposal in our first meeting together.

Angelo's Story

I didn't start working in libraries until I was thirty. I came to this profession after just over a decade of moving from job to job and place to place. Coming to librarianship felt like coming home. The people who raised me taught me two important values: solidarity and intellectual curiosity. Library work fits easily with those values: I was helping people explore their own curiosity and interests, and there was no monetary transaction involved. After several years of library work, it became clear to me that another value I learned growing up would also apply to my experience: resistance to injustice. I could see that things were and had been changing in the library world, tilting toward workplace injustices that would ultimately degrade our profession and harm our patrons. Higher wages were directed to the few top administrative positions while the mass of public-facing librarians and library workers were being devalued. At East Lansing Public Library in Michigan, we formed a union for many reasons. What I remain most proud of is the fact that our union stopped this race to the bottom in our library. Our contract won higher compensation and better protections for our most vulnerable but most visible and patron-centered workers.

Emily's Story

In 2008 I found myself in a faculty and staff meeting at the small private college where I worked as a reference librarian, discussing what to do with an unexpected budget surplus. Administration wanted community feedback: should we spend these funds boosting faculty salaries, or spread the funds equally across the two job categories? Faculty argued strongly that the surplus should go to them. Their salaries were low for the New York City metro area. Faculty argued that the school would be unable to hire quality teachers at numbers that low. I could feel the steam coming out of my ears. They weren't wrong. They also made at least $25,000 more than I did as a professional librarian, and I knew I made $15,000 more than the lowest paid workers in my shop. Faculty ended up voting to keep the surplus for themselves.

Later that year I landed a new position as a faculty librarian at Long Island University, Brooklyn. The school has a rich union history. The Long Island University Faculty Federation was the first private higher education union in the country and had a history of taking labor action, including striking, to secure better wages and working conditions. My salary instantly increased by $25,000 and my annual leave tripled. It was the union difference. I went on strike with that union in 2011 and was locked out in 2016. Both experiences persuaded me that collective action is a necessary precursor to justice. I have been working on behalf of both ever since.

Kelly's Story

A few years before I started working at Oregon State University, there had been a deeply unpopular (and possibly unnecessary) round of furloughs during a period of financial uncertainty. At the time faculty had to just sit and take it, although the anger about these furloughs helped fuel the work of our local Association of American University Professors chapter, which ultimately evolved into our union, United Academics Oregon State University. Fast forward to 2020: our new union completed bargaining our first contract early during the COVID-19 pandemic when enrollment and funding uncertainties were especially high. Once again our salaries were on the line, but this time we were able to bargain over the administration's proposal: we had a say in what happened. We insisted that the cuts only be implemented if university finances actually required them and that money would be given back if it ultimately wasn't needed. We made the cuts more progressive, limiting the impact on the most vulnerable. And at the very end of our negotiations, in a 26-hour marathon session, we discovered that the administration had failed to account for the reduction in retirement contributions—so we were able to reduce the proposed cuts *by 25 percent* and still end up with the savings that the administration said they needed.

Without a union, those cuts could have simply been applied as they were originally proposed, without recourse or scrutiny. However, this time we had a union and were at the table. I often think about this story when someone tells me that management has a bird's-eye view of what happens in the workplace and that they're paid a premium because they know best. While we were there to represent the interests of our bargaining unit, we also offered another set of eyes and minds to solve the problems of our workplace. When management feels threatened by workers being informed and involved in workplace decision-making, it tells me that they're more afraid of being caught being wrong than ready to accept help getting things right.

Meredith's Story

In the spring of 2017, I drove to a casino in Detroit to attend the American Federation of Teachers National Higher Education Conference. The event caught my eye because Tressie McMillan Cottom was a keynote speaker. I had recently read (and greatly enjoyed) McMillan Cottom's book *Lower Ed: The Troubling Rise of For-Profit Colleges in the New Economy*, and the chance to see her speak seemed too good to pass up. That same day I also saw Jane McAlevey give a plenary session about how to build a strong union, and I heard Emily discuss her experiences during the lockout at Long Island University. I ate lunch with a group of union organizers and fellow union members from higher ed locals scattered throughout the state. I came home with a lot of ideas. But it would take some time for those ideas to bear fruit.

In the summer of 2020, the Regents of the University of Michigan approved a neutrality policy meant to ease the creation of new unions on our campus, and at the same time my colleagues and I were feeling the effects of pandemic-era austerity measures. This combination of events created a unique opportunity, and a group of us saw the potential for change. We formed an organizing committee, made a list, and talked to everyone we could reach. After going public with a union card campaign in February 2021, we reached a majority in a matter of weeks. Just like workers at East Lansing Public Library, the librarians, archivists, and curators at the University of Michigan chose to form a union for a variety of reasons. But perhaps most important, the pandemic had shown us that working for a prestigious and well-resourced employer was not sufficient protection for our salaries and our jobs and did not guarantee us a seat at the table when important decisions were made.

Introduction

※

We believe that the most effective strategy for building our collective power as library workers—for the good of our profession, its institutions, and our patrons—is unionization. Winning a union is not easy, but we have a rich history of experiences and lessons from which to draw inspiration and advice. This history comes not only from the library workers who came before us, but also from all workers everywhere who have understood and acted on the conviction that there is power in a union. We believe that you, too, can have a union. This book is meant to present you with those experiences and lessons so that, together with your coworkers, you can apply them and win.

About This Book

We have organized the book into chapters that cover the biggest topics for getting started with your union, or for getting involved in your existing union. We begin the book by telling you what unions are and why you need them. If you don't have a union, it can feel overwhelming to know how to start. Most working people are not members of unions (yet!), and in fact, though their popularity has increased, and workers are winning union elections at unprecedented rates (Glass, 2024), overall union membership has been on the decline for decades. It's no wonder you might not know where to begin. In Chapter 2 we'll give you some direction for getting started with organizing, and in Chapter 3 we will walk through the steps of getting a new union rolling. The labor movement is composed of all sorts of workers from all sorts of industries, and we have much more in common with each other than management might have you think. But library workers do have some particularities that we will discuss in detail in Chapter 4. In Chapter 5 we'll focus on campaigns, the concrete ways you and your coworkers will fight for the changes you want to see in your working lives and beyond. In Chapters 6 and 7 we'll talk about how you can win big changes on the job through a written contract called a collective bargaining agreement and how to enforce that contract through constant engagement with the bosses. Finally, in Chapter 8 we'll offer you our own vision for the future of libraries and the role that our mighty unions play in bringing about that future. Following this is a bonus chapter for bosses. If you've made it this far and you're the boss—a library director, supervisor, middle manager, or in a position of authority in your library workplace—please know that our vision for the future does not exclude leadership or condemn administrative acumen. On the contrary, we believe a good understanding of and relationship to the organic institution built by the workers at your library will make your work life more rewarding and meaningful.

Please note that there will be many specifics that we do not cover in any given chapter—this book is intended as a starting place, not an ending to your research. However, each chapter includes basic definitions and an overview of the topic, as well as our broad recommendations.

As you read this book, you will encounter an intimidating number of acronyms that describe union affiliations. We have chosen to render the names of many unions and their parent organizations using just their acronyms rather than spelling out their full names. Unions that have been around a long time often took their names from the first groups of workers they organized and represented. But today the United Auto Workers, the International Association of Machinists, and the American Federation of Teachers all represent workers in a variety of industries, and spelling out the full name of AFSCME or SEIU doesn't automatically tell you much about the workers they represent. As you learn more about the relationships between an individual bargaining unit, a "local," and an "international," these acronyms will become less confusing. Until then, think of them as shorthand for quickly describing the larger body with which any individual union is affiliated.

Throughout the book you'll encounter stories from library workers who are members and leaders of their unions. We conducted group and individual interviews during the summer of 2023, talking with school, academic, and public library workers and on specific issues, including collective bargaining, grievances and arbitration, and organizing a new union. We hope that their thoughts on strategy, practice, and values will help inform your perspective. There is no one way to run a union, and taking in many views is part of the work of unionists. Unions are formal institutions, and they do not inherently or necessarily always do the right thing or behave the way that we want them to. They are as strong and as good and strategic as we can make them, through hard work and political struggle. We hope these stories inspire you to talk to other workers, in libraries and beyond. Parts of this book may make you uncomfortable or make you reconsider your assumptions about work, libraries, and power. You may find parts too radical—or not radical enough! This book is just one entry to thinking about organized labor in libraries, and we encourage you to keep reading and learning beyond it. Although this book builds from our own experiences, it does not represent our individual unions or employers, and the same is true for the stories shared by library unionists throughout the book.

Chapters 1-8 each end with an Action Plan to help you move forward in your own organizing. Organizing is an *active* activity: you'll need to read, think, talk, and do in order to build power with other workers. Each Action Plan includes a few suggested readings, some questions for reflection, and some assignments—activities to help you deepen your knowledge, broaden your network, and practice important skills. You may notice similarities across these plans—yes, we will ask you to talk to your coworkers, again and again, about what you all care about changing and what you're willing to do to change it. This is how we build and maintain a strong union. We encourage you to use the Action Plan with your comrades: bring an activity to a union meeting or ask a few coworkers to read an article with you. While it might feel strange to use a term like *comrade*, we have chosen this word deliberately, as it has a long history (going back to the 1880s!) as a term of address for people who are committed to making change together. Comrade implies a sense of shared values and a shared desire to make change based on those values. We hope you have many comrades among your coworkers.

What Is a Union and Why Do I Need One?

> Unionization carries a higher emotional charge than most library issues.
> —Bernard Berelson (1939, p. 477)
>
> I want this to be an example for library workers across the state. If we come together and fight for what you and the community deserve, we can win!
> —Tori Patrick, library worker and executive board member for Daniel Boone Regional Library Workers United (DBRLWU), AFSCME Council 61, quoted in a press release (Fernandez, 2023) after DBRLWU ratified their first contract

Forming a union is the most effective way for workers to shape the conditions of a workplace. When workers organize themselves into a union, they can collectively negotiate the terms and conditions of their jobs. Without a union, individual workers are left to negotiate those terms on their own, with no guarantee there will even be an opportunity to negotiate. In a unionized workplace, the opportunities to adjust working conditions are built into the structure of the institution itself. In nonunionized workplaces, to the extent that these opportunities exist, they are made available only by the unilateral whim of the bosses. Simply put, without a union, workers have nothing. With a union, workers have the opportunity to get something. In this chapter we introduce basic terminology and concepts, offer some historical context for labor unions in libraries, and end with a discussion of why a union is so powerful and what it can do for you.

Terms to Know

A *union* is what we often call any group of workers who use their collective power to shape the conditions of their labor. Simply put, a union is you and your coworkers coming together to advocate for your shared interests. When certified and recognized as the exclusive bargaining agent for a group of workers, unions have the legal right to negotiate as equals with employers about a variety of issues in the workplace (Prosten, 2020, p. 259). A frequently negotiated issue is wages, but negotiations are far from limited to this topic. In fact many see unions as the "only real way to have a real say in their workplaces and in their professions" (Prosten, 2020, p. 260). The important thing to remember is that you are the union. A union is not some far-away organization that you send money to in exchange for services on your behalf, but rather the "collective experience of workers in struggle" (McAlevey, 2016, p. v). This collective experience can be powerful, and the extent to which you build and use your collective power will determine your ability to succeed in winning the changes you want.

The relationship between workers and management reflects a *structured antagonism*, where the interests of both sides are set up to be in conflict and the "worker" and the "boss" stand in for larger, more complex dynamics in the workplace (Dundon et al., 2017). Considering this structured antagonism helps clarify that management takes action on behalf of their interests, which do not necessarily align with the interests of workers. The union becomes a mechanism for workers to take action on behalf of their own interests—and it is only natural that there is conflict.

Almost all unionized workplaces feature at least one *collective bargaining agreement*, often referred to as a CBA or simply the *contract*. This contract is an agreement between workers and their employer about wages, benefits, hours, and other working conditions. Contracts typically last a specified number of years. Most contracts also contain language defining the positions covered in the agreement. The full group of those positions is referred to as a *bargaining unit*. Some libraries might have several bargaining units and therefore several contracts. This is often the case when there are supervisory and nonsupervisory units, each with their own CBA. We'll talk more about how this happens in Chapters 4 and 7.

Perhaps the most important thing a union accomplishes is a fundamental change in the nature of your relationship with your employer. With the protections of a strong contract, you are no longer an at-will employee. *At-will employees* can be fired for any reason—or no reason at all. Nearly all contracts include articles that describe provisions for discipline and dismissal as well as layoff and recall. Although it can be scary to think about these topics, the contract provides tools for protecting workers in difficult situations.

A good contract will establish *just cause* and *progressive discipline*, which mandate that disciplinary actions must be grounded in fact (not capricious) and appropriate in nature (proportional to the offense). Along with contract language regarding discrimination and harassment, these provisions can help ensure that workers are treated equitably. For example, most contracts would prevent a worker from being fired for a single instance of showing up late for a shift, and if a boss wants to discipline a worker for poor performance, the employee typically has the opportunity to demonstrate improvement before any further disciplinary action can occur.

While employers have a duty to uphold their end of the bargain when it comes to your contract, there will come a time when a worker's rights are violated or the terms of the CBA are not respected. This is why every good contract also includes procedures for *grievances* and *arbitration*. When the employer fails to meet their obligations and the union seeks redress, this process takes the form of a grievance, a set of procedures to adjudicate an alleged violation. If a grievance cannot ultimately be resolved between the union and the employer, the union can pursue arbitration, which allows for a third party to hear the case and render a binding decision. Think about it: management no longer has the final say on whether something is right or wrong at work. As concepts, progressive discipline, just cause, and grievances and arbitration may seem rather abstract. However, these are some of the most important tools a union can use to secure and maintain the rights of workers.

A Brief Historical Interlude

Library workers have been a part of the labor movement for a long time. Female librarians at the New York Public Library founded the first union for public library workers in 1917 to fight discriminatory hiring practices faced by women in their ranks (Milden, 1977). While the formation of public library unions in Boston, Philadelphia, and Washington, DC, quickly followed, anti-union activism successfully painted union supporters as "irresponsible fanatics" who endangered the "genteel occupation" of professional librarians (Milden, 1977, p. 153). These appeals to professionalism and the nobility of our work sound strangely familiar to twenty-first-century ears, and their historical effectiveness helps us understand why they are still among the anti-union rhetoric we hear today. None of these early unions survived, and some public library systems saw the dissolution and reorganization of successive unions over the course of decades (Guyton, 1975).

As a record of a professional organization making its way through the tail end of the Great Depression, the American Library Association (ALA) secretary's report of 1937 is a fascinating read. The association's long-serving leader Carl H. Milam describes phenomena that will no doubt be familiar to today's library workers:

> Salaries, low by any standard, qualifications considered, have not kept pace with the rising cost of living or with salaries in other professions. . . . Library employees, along with most other intelligent employed persons, are perhaps feeling the urge to demand not only better working conditions and salaries which will support a higher standard of living, but also more economic security and a larger part in the control of the destinies and policies of the agencies or institutions with which they are associated. Surely it is not too much to hope that the directors of libraries, when facing these issues, will recall that the modern library movement was reared in the liberal democratic tradition. (Milam, 1937, p. 488)

Like our colleagues of the 1930s, today's library workers also find themselves struggling with stagnant wages, difficult working conditions, and threats to the existence of libraries themselves.

Reading a 1939 *Library Quarterly* article detailing a period of renewed interest in unionization in the library sector, we learn that public library workers in Butte, Montana, formed a union in 1934 "after the library board had voted to close the library because of lack of funds" (Berelson, 1939, p. 499). But unions were not the only solution proposed to benefit libraries and (purportedly) their workers. During this era of post-Depression union activity, libraries themselves encouraged the formation of "staff associations," whose aim was to "be organized along constructive lines, stressing particularly the aim of cooperation with the library authorities, rather than by emphasizing 'rights' in an antagonistic spirit" (Nourse, 1934, p. 873). Functioning in a manner akin to "company unions," these staff associations lacked the ability to meaningfully address wages and working conditions because they existed at the pleasure of management, and instead they served as social and professional support (Berelson, 1939; Guyton, 1975).

In the postwar period, changes in state laws regarding collective bargaining spurred the formation of many new library unions. University of California (UC) Berkeley librarians were among the first academic librarians at a public institution to unionize in 1965 (Phillips et al., 2019), and by the summer of 1971 the community would see not one but two labor actions by library unions. In June, twenty librarians—members of the University Federation of Librarians, AFT Local 1795—participated in a university-wide strike, joining their union siblings in a fight over wages. On the picket line, the police sprayed two of them with mace, and one was sent to the hospital. They later won a 10 percent raise (Eshelman, 1972). In August of that same year, staff and librarians of the Berkeley Public Library went out on a two-day strike and were the first-ever Berkeley city employees to strike. The workers won a 5 percent wage increase and later successfully fought efforts to eliminate library hours on Sundays (Guyton, 1975).

The more that library employees join with other workers, the more power they'll have to improve their own working conditions and compensation. Take for example the aforementioned UC Berkeley strike. Because librarians participated in the strike, and were even attacked and injured by police on the picket line, they gained the trust and camaraderie of other groups of workers on campus. This battle-tested solidarity led to material gains for the librarians. According to Laurel Burley, a member of the library worker union:

> No one sold anybody out and indeed in the last marathon bargaining session some seven hours were spent with the University offering the building trades a few more dollars if they would forget about the librarians' low salaries, a sell-out the building trades refused to listen to. (Eshelman, 1972, p. 133)

This brief history shows that library workers have long come together to support their own rights and the very libraries they work in. As we return to the present, it is important to ground ourselves in the espoused values of our profession. The fifth statement of the ALA's Code of Ethics (American Library Association [ALA] Committee on Professional Ethics, 2021) declares that library workers should be guided by the principle that "we treat co-workers and other colleagues with respect, fairness, and good faith, and advocate conditions of employment that safeguard the rights and welfare of all employees of our institutions." The ninth states that library workers "confront inequity and oppression" (ALA Committee on Professional Ethics, 2021). This book takes these principles seriously and further argues that to make them a reality, library workers should organize themselves into unions in order to make positive and long-lasting structural changes in their workplaces. The collective bargaining power of library workers is the best way to safeguard our rights and welfare on the job. This power is much stronger than simply relying on the "potentially retractable beneficence of individuals" who occupy unelected positions of power in the profession (Ferndale Area District Library Workers Union, 2022).

Why Do You Need a Union?

Have you ever asked for a raise? Maybe your boss said it wasn't the right time. Have you ever found out that a colleague with less experience made more than you do? Maybe your boss said it was impolite to talk about other people's salaries. Did you feel taken advantage of when your work was deemed essential during the pandemic, but your pay didn't change? Did you feel like you didn't have a voice when decisions were made in your workplace? If these things have happened to you, you're not alone. A union can negotiate for better pay, improved benefits, and a more humane workplace. Are you paid less than your colleagues at a nearby library despite a higher cost of living in your area? Has your pay failed to keep pace with inflation? Has the cost of your healthcare been increasing year after year? At the bargaining table, you have the opportunity to tell your employer how these economic realities affect you, and your boss can't decline to talk about these topics.

While we tend to focus on the financial aspects of what a union can do, it's important to remember that our workplaces can be inequitable in other ways too. Have you ever been written up for something minor? Maybe you found out later that your coworkers aren't held to the same standard. Have you ever felt unsafe around a particular patron, but your boss said to suck it up? Maybe after that interaction you didn't feel comfortable talking to your boss about these issues. At the bargaining table, you can talk about equity and safety in the workplace, and your boss can't ignore your concerns.

For as long as there have been both unions and libraries, library workers have joined unions. The motivations have changed over time, and union density within the profession has fluctuated. Some earlier motivations for joining unions included maintaining the professional status and job security of librarians, resisting undesirable work, and winning more leave time (Higbee, 1982). Although the question of who benefits from unionization often elicits answers that distinguish between professional librarians and their staff colleagues (Applegate, 2009), we take the view that unions can and should serve the interests of all library workers and are a tool for transforming our workplaces.

The need for such transformation is clear. In 2017 Jo Henry, Joe Eshleman, and Richard Moniz's book *The Dysfunctional Library: Challenges and Solutions to Workplace Relationships* was published, giving legitimacy and a name to widespread experiences of dissatisfaction in the library workplace. This sense of dissatisfaction is not limited to working conditions but extends to the library itself as an organization. A few years later, building off the work of Henry et al., Routledge published an edited collection titled *Libraries as Dysfunctional Organizations and Workplaces.* This book attempted to further examine the concept of dysfunction as it applies to libraries as organizations, to generalize observations from an individual or psychological level to a broader socio-organizational level, and to look for solutions.

Widespread discontent is evident in library workplaces, and research has provided us with identifiable reasons for this discontent. The topics identified as most prevalent in library and information science scholarship about library dysfunction all fall squarely within the realm of labor organizing: "low morale, burnout, and turnover; problematic recruitment, retention, and hiring practices; discrimination and lack of workforce diversity, equity, and inclusion; and incivility, harassment, and bullying" (Acadia & Vogt, 2023, p. 15). Research has also demonstrated that even the systems put in place to address dysfunction can exacerbate experiences of abuse and neglect, particularly for library workers of color (Davis Kendrick & Damasco, 2019; Davis Kendrick, 2021). Although not everyone agrees on a solution, dozens of library workers from across the country asserted in interviews with us that unions can combat dysfunction in the workplace. Unsurprisingly, there is widespread interest in unionization, as demonstrated by the successful election campaign of Emily, an open unionist, to the presidency of ALA in 2022 and indeed by the association's decision to publish this book.

We can only build strong libraries by building our capacity as organized library workers. This means developing governing skills ourselves. We do not believe that all library workers all of the time possess the skill or the willingness to govern the library, but all library workers all of the time have the potential to learn how and be willing to govern the library. And we bring many skills from our work and lived experiences, from research and working with the public to negotiating with vendors to navigating challenging politics of funding and advocacy. Many of our existing skills translate well to labor organizing. This is true even in states that limit collective bargaining and other tactics for unions. As Maria, a member of United Faculty of Florida at the University of North Florida put it, "How do we mobilize? We can't strike; we can't really do much of anything. We could talk to the press, but buttons were a big thing. And that was my outreach librarian know-how: I'm gonna buy a button machine." Each library worker knows something about their role at the library and probably feels a certain way about their compensation and treatment. What is our job and how do we do it? How do we feel about it, and what would we like to change? Do we feel we are justly compensated and that we are treated fairly? The more we reflect on these questions, the more knowledge and awareness we build toward imagining a stronger, better library.

Recently formed library worker unions advocate not just for better working conditions at their libraries but also for strengthening libraries themselves. The workers at Howard County (Maryland) Library System argue that a living wage enables better service to the community and allows the library to "recruit and retain diverse, highly-qualified staff" (HoCo Library Workers United, 2023). Cate Levinson, a union leader at the Niles-Maine District Library, argues that the union makes the library stronger as a whole and that "with fairer wages and better treatment, the library workers that our community knows and trusts are more likely to stay" (Requena, 2023).

Organizing our libraries will require confrontation with a default orientation among private- and public-sector employers to resist the unionization of nearly all workplaces and with the inherited authoritarian structures and practices of library governance and management. Organizing aims to build—from the bottom up—the confidence, capacity, and power of library workers to develop alternative forms of governance that promote a librarianship that fully embodies its declared egalitarian principles (ALA Committee on Professional Ethics, 2021).

The strength of a union can be measured by the level of participation of the workers who belong to it. A strong union is one that successfully directs the collective wisdom and experience of its members toward library governance. Unfortunately, library systems have inherited organizational structures that stunt and impede this collective power by restricting decisions to a small minority of individuals, many of whom may rarely step out of their offices long enough to understand much about how library workers deliver services and keep the library functioning on a day-to-day basis. Library workers of all ranks care deeply about the work we do and often genuinely want the best for our libraries. We have insight and opinions about how things are going, and how they might go better, at our worksites. Rather than allow for this deep wisdom and commitment to flourish, our outdated, top-down, hierarchical structures have stifled and frustrated the great mass of wisdom and power that sits at the bottom of our organizational charts—where, it should be said, a great number of Black, Indigenous, and people of color workers reside. By building up the power of all library workers through unions, we seek to build up the full, untapped potential of libraries themselves.

It will not be possible to unionize every library without the hard work, commitment, dedication, and discipline required to organize. It is comfortable and easy to imagine that your coworkers will unionize based on the force of reason and common interest. It is tempting to believe that you must like the people you organize with or that your most likely allies are the ones who are most vocal about equality and social justice. Although reason and common interest matter, and while you will find strength in those with whom you share a common political vision, it will not be possible to achieve the kind of bottom-up power necessary to confront our adversaries and transform our profession without building lists, identifying and recruiting leaders, identifying issues, making plans to win, and inviting every single one of your coworkers—even the ones you don't get along with—to participate in the plan. Not all unions are the same, and none of them are perfect. But the general principles and goals of organized labor can bring us closer to our patrons and our coworkers and can improve the overall strength of our libraries.

Library workers must lead the transformation of library workplaces. Library workers must get organized, and that starts by having intentional, thoughtful conversations with coworkers. It involves getting to know what matters to them, discovering who the workplace leaders are, and asking each other to take the necessary but hard steps toward creating the kinds of workplaces we want and deserve. Building collective power means expanding the possibilities for change, in our workplaces and in our communities, and the next chapter will describe how to begin. Starting a union will not solve all the problems in library worksites, but it is among the most powerful tools available to make transformation possible.

Action Plan
Ask Yourself

- What are your personal assumptions about unions? Think about your own union story—this might include current or past working experience with a union, family or friends' experiences, or memories of a picket line at a local business.
- What would you like to change about your working conditions? Have you tried talking to other workers about these issues? Do they share your concerns?

Readings

McAlevey, J. (2016). The power to win is in the community, not the boardroom. In *No shortcuts: Organizing for power in the new Gilded Age*. Oxford University Press.

Wallman, S. (2022). *Our members be unlimited: A comic about workers and their unions*. Scribe Publications.

Assignment

Talk to a friend or acquaintance about their union. How does it work? What do they like about it? What would they like to change? How does their union affect their working life? Getting to know your union "cousins" across other organizations and even other fields can help you contextualize the labor struggle and build a network of support.

How Do We Start?

> The idea is that it's a ladder, like a ladder up and down, right? So maybe you just show up to a union lunch. And if I see someone who has shown up to a union lunch, oh, I remember I talked with you and maybe I can ask you for this thing. So it's like networking, like who shows up. Also, if I've heard from you because you're mad about something that I did, I will frequently ask you to serve. If you cared enough to bend my ear about that, then maybe you have some passion. And maybe from experience with union work, you'll understand the nuances of multiple perspectives, right?
>
> —Emily, librarian at Portland State University (PSU) and president of PSU American Association of University Professors

For many of us in the library profession, working in a unionized environment is new, something we may be learning about for the first time. And that's no accident. In 1947 after a wave of postwar labor unrest that saw as many as five million Americans engaged in strike action, federal legislators moved to restrict union power as a way of securing labor peace. Over the veto of President Harry S. Truman, Congress passed the Taft-Hartley Act, legislation that amended the National Labor Relations Act to prohibit a range of union activities that contribute to worker power including wildcat strikes (strikes that take place without official union authorization), solidarity strikes (when workers strike on behalf of other striking workers rather than against their own management), economic boycotts, and union contributions to political campaigns (intended to dilute state support for organized labor). Taken together, Taft-Hartley greatly reduced the capacity of workers to organize with each other to secure higher wages and better working conditions.

Federal legislation weakening the power of unions spurred many states to pass similar bills. The years following the passage of Taft-Hartley saw the rise of so-called *right-to-work* laws that limit the ability of unions to fund their work through union dues. (We will discuss the ramifications of these laws in more depth in Chapter 4.) Federal law prohibited *closed shops*, or workplaces that require all workers to join the union, but did allow *agency shops*. In an agency shop, workers are not required to join the union. Because they receive the benefits of the union through the contract negotiated on their behalf, unions could require an *agency fee* in recognition of the service provided. Generally the agency fee would match the cost of dues paid by union members. The agency fee recognizes that, member or not, all workers who benefit from the wages and working conditions collectively bargained by their union should contribute to the costs of those efforts. Like any institution, the union requires funds to run, from the salaries of union staff who may administer grievances, support organizing, and keep the books, to signs and buttons for the picket line, and everything in between. In right-to-work states, agency fees are generally prohibited, thereby weakening the union by reducing its resources. In 2018 the Supreme Court ruled in *Janus v. AFSCME* that public sector workers could not be compelled to pay an agency fee. Though private sector unions can still require the agency fee in states without right-to-work laws, under *Janus v. AFSCME* all public sector workers face an uphill battle to build and maintain power.

In 2023 polling showed that an impressive 67 percent of people in the United States approved of unions, which "marks the fifth straight year this reading has exceeded its long-term average of 62%" (Saad, 2023). Despite this level of support, the number of workers who actually belong to a union is abysmally low. In 2023 the union membership rate in the United States was only 10 percent (US Bureau of Labor Statistics, 2024). Within libraries the statistics are a bit higher—16 percent of library technicians and 27 percent of librarians were unionized in 2023 (Hirsch et al., 2024). This means that although you may want a union at your library, it is very likely that there are not many, or any, unionized workers in your life whom you can go to for advice and information. You might not have any idea about where and how to get started. Although that may feel intimidating, don't let it stop you! Maty, Boston Public Library Professional Staff Association, Massachusetts Library Staff Association, AFT Local 4928, reminded us that we were never trained for this and that the only people who don't make mistakes are people who "don't know shit." They advised readers that you will learn as you go and to be kind to yourself and not beat yourself up. We find this a helpful reminder as we discuss how to get started building or rebuilding your union.

Building Worker Power

Building worker power starts with *organizing*: getting people to take action together. This section covers a few of the important actions that library workers must take in order to organize their workplace. It all starts with talking to your coworkers. Then you'll want to identify leaders and discover the most important issues people want to address. You and your coworkers will come up with a plan to address those issues, and you'll ask each other to participate directly in implementing the plan. If you do not yet have a union at your library, your first plan should be to win a union. However, the organizing principles discussed in this chapter can apply to a variety of efforts to build worker power at the library, not just winning a union. You may use these skills to drive momentum around an issue campaign or to revitalize a stagnant union. (See the story in Chapter 5 about workers who democratized their union.) Or you may work in a state where public employees cannot legally form unions or where you cannot negotiate a contract—you can still use organizing to build power and strategize a plan to make change in your workplace.

Talking to Your Coworkers

The foundation of a strong group of organized library workers is face-to-face, intentional conversations. These conversations help you learn about the experiences of your coworkers and find out what they would like to change at work. These conversations will be most successful if you listen more than you speak. (A common union saying points out that you have two ears and only one mouth.) Ask as many questions as possible to help your coworkers identify and explain the issue or issues that they care deeply about. You will help them understand that they have the power to address those issues when they join with their coworkers to demand change. It is also important that you invite them to consider the potential consequences of taking collective action on the job.

These conversations should always include an *ask*—something that you're inviting the other person to commit to. Library workers are not strangers to these types of conversations. Those of us who work directly with patrons, connecting them to library resources, know that in order to be successful, we have to ask good questions and do a lot of listening. Our goal when we talk to patrons in a reference interview is to discover the specific need they have and how we might be able to meet that need using our library resources and our own skills.

Our goal when we talk to our coworkers is to discover what problems they feel strongly about and invite them to take collective action to solve those problems.

These conversations aren't only about business—they're also about building relationships. We spoke with dozens of library workers who confirmed this. Katie, librarian at the Westland Public Library in Michigan, SEIU 517M, shared, "The first advice that I would give people is just never act alone. That seems like it could be obvious, but it's not obvious. The point of a union is that it's a group project. It's connection. As adrienne maree brown says in her work, *Emergent Strategy*, 'move at the speed of trust.' If you don't have trust with your colleagues who you're trying to organize, you are not going anywhere. So start getting in good with your colleagues . . . be people first, be colleagues first. Be comrades first. Tell inside jokes first."

Although the specifics will vary based on your relationship with the other person, the three parts of an organizing conversation come down to a common labor slogan: agitate, educate, and organize.

Agitate may sound negative, but it really means digging in with your listening. Typically any organizing conversation will start with broad questions: *Tell me about your work! What's going on in your branch these days?* Agitating means listening to what is under the surface. Sometimes it is clear: a worker may tell you that the power keeps going out or scheduling is a nightmare. However, many of us are socialized not to complain openly and may not immediately be upfront about problems. A worker with the same scheduling issues may just say that everyone seems extra busy these days. Agitation often looks like follow-up questions: *That doesn't seem fair. Does that happen to everyone?*

Educate is about connecting these issues to a broader context. It may mean comparison with other libraries—when pay is the big issue, it helps to point out the union advantage, and this is even more successful when you can give examples of a union's effectiveness in your region or community. It may also mean connecting to the broader labor struggle, noting that workers at other libraries or other workplaces have won protections over similar issues.

Organize means making an ask. It's about getting the person to decide if they'll commit to one next step: it could be to attend a meeting, talk to another coworker, or put up three posters around campus. It's important that the ask is reasonable—you wouldn't ask someone new to go talk to every single person in their department, for example. In addition, there has to be a plan for follow up: *I'll see you at the meeting* or *We can have coffee, and you can tell me what your coworkers said*. Often the asks that make up organizing are part of how we actually get things done in our unions: it takes a bunch of people telling three coworkers to end up with a full meeting or to get all the posters put up, or whatever else the goal is. Asks also typically build over time. Someone who has talked to one coworker may be willing to talk to two or three next time or take on more complex or difficult tasks.

This process isn't automatic! It makes sense to start with conversations that you expect to go well, but also be ready to take advantage of moments that present themselves. A few of our library unionists shared stories of their first organizing conversations:

- Ginny, Faculty Alliance of Miami (AAUP/AFT): "My first organizing conversation with librarians was with my really good friend and colleague. We were just sitting on my couch. We were writing an article and I was like, *Hey, I've got a question for you.* And we just kind of snaked our tendrils out from there to talk to all of the other librarians. But it obviously worked. We got a unanimous vote to form our union, 90% turnout."
- Becca, Northwestern University Library Workers Union, SEIU Local 73: "The first organizing conversation I had was also not typical because I was on a walk with a work friend and she said something like, *Well if there were a union here . . .* And I was like, *Well, actually, if you're interested in that, there's a group of us who are starting to organize.* But after that, it really ran the gamut. There were some people who said, *Yes, absolutely.* Some people were initially opposed and we had to have many organizing conversations with them, and there's one person who's now on the bargaining committee who was originally assessed as being anti-union at the beginning, which is great."

Ginny and Becca both had their first conversations with friends—people they had built trust and natural rapport with. You won't be able to do that with everyone, of course—in order to build a strong union, you'll need to talk to *everyone*, even the brand new person, that shy person who likes to keep to themselves, that person who always seems really grumpy, and yes, even that person that you don't particularly like. Think of it as a challenge to know a little more about everyone you work with—and you will often be surprised by what you find.

In every organizing conversation, you will learn something. Often workers share information about their work—problems or things that work well—and you'll learn what that particular person cares about. You may also learn that someone is anti-union or deeply skeptical of unions. Many unions have ways to share the information you've gleaned with other activists or staff, for example, so that the grievance chair can follow up about a potential grievance or that, when the labor-management taskforce about childcare gets going, you can make sure to invite people who care about that issue to join; if someone has made it clear they don't want to hear from you again, you can note that as well. Many unions use a 4- or 5-point scale to assess each conversation, for example, with 1 meaning that someone is actively involved in organizing and 4 or 5 meaning they're strongly anti-union and may even be actively working against the union. This is part of preparing for *structure tests*, which assess the strength of your union. If your group consists mostly of 3s—people on the fence but certainly not active—it isn't a good time to do a really visible action. If people aren't willing to wear a union button or sign a public petition, they're unlikely to do more escalatory actions. On the other hand, structure tests can also help workers see that they're not alone. Often once people see how many of their coworkers have signed on, it makes it less intimidating to do so themselves. Keeping updated assessments also ensures you have current information—someone who was a big supporter but disappeared may need you to check in with them. Like Becca says, we've all seen 4s who end up becoming 1s in full support of the union—it may not be common, but it certainly happens.

Still it can be painful to have hard conversations with your coworkers. When you go into a conversation, remember that it isn't personal. There may be people you like who don't support the union or people you really don't like who do. Your coworkers may say things that seem misguided or hurtful, or they may have internalized misconceptions about unions. You will want to be prepared with points to correct misinformation, but know that you will not convince everyone. One of the strengths of one-on-one organizing over time is that you can develop relationships and keep coming back to the conversation. It is better if your coworker can honestly say no to you rather than say yes today but not actually follow through with their commitment. Keep in mind that even coworkers who refuse to help are covered by the contract, and the union represents everyone in the bargaining unit.

The Importance of Inoculation

Taking the side of workers is much more difficult than taking the side of bosses. The contemporary workplace is structured as an authoritarian regime, and there is a real risk to standing up to the bosses, especially in a country where losing one's job can mean losing one's access to, among other things, healthcare, housing, or a legal right to reside in the United States. Voicing your disagreements with management can invite retaliation (read more on this in Chapter 7), and bosses might make your work life uncomfortable, unpleasant, or even unbearable. In our profession, as in many, advancement and career mobility often depend on the good word of the bosses. This has created a culture of deference to authority and practices of self-censorship. It is important to remember that these fears are real and that a good organizer will validate and speak frankly about them.

Fear is often expressed as apathy. Our profession is largely dedicated to public service and to upholding institutions that are widely revered by the general population. It is unlikely that library workers are genuinely apathetic about library services and working conditions. Many of us were motivated to work in libraries because we care deeply about them and the people they serve. But when you talk to your fellow library workers about work, you might find that though they can identify a myriad of problems that need solving, they seem uninterested in exploring possible solutions. A good organizer recognizes that this attitude is not really apathy; it is fear.

It's not easy to get rid of fear. We have probably all worked somewhere where management rules by fear. A fearful workforce is sometimes a structural necessity created by management. It is one of the many ways that the bosses keep us disorganized and unwilling to confront bad behavior. A good organizer does not attempt to eradicate this fear. A good organizer instead "taps into righteous anger about workplace injustices" and helps coworkers find "the courage and determination to act" (Bradbury et al., 2016, p. 9). *Inoculation* is an important part of an organizing conversation, where you specifically address fears and prepare your colleague for the potential responses of management.

Know Your Rights

As organizers we spend a lot of time on inoculation because sometimes the bad stuff we are afraid will happen actually does. In Chapter 5, you'll read the story of five public library workers who were fired in the midst of organizing a union. That particular story has a hopeful and happy ending, and the workers eventually won both their union and a strong contract. But they were only able to do so because they were willing to take risks. Much of the work of building power in your workplace—organizing a union, winning a fair contract, and enforcing that contract—will require you to publicly assert your rights. In the course of this work, you will find yourself engaging in activities like circulating and signing petitions, holding a march or rally, or speaking to the press. For many of us, exercising our rights to speak freely, to assemble, and to associate with others in the service of collective action might feel uncomfortable or scary at first. But doing these things is how we win.

You have a right to talk to your coworkers about your wages, hours, and working conditions. You have a right to speak publicly about what is happening in your workplace. You have a right to object to and even to protest the actions of your employer. You have a right to demand better treatment and to seek redress when harm occurs. The details of precisely how we exercise these rights can be complicated and vary based on where we live and where we work, and it is advisable to take time to understand the legal landscape that applies specifically to you and your coworkers. But just because something is complicated or scary is not a reason to avoid doing it. As Tara, a public library worker and an officer for Worthington Public Libraries United (WPLU), Ohio Federation of Teachers Local 6606, explained, she approached organizing with both caution and bravery:

> I talked to my family, and I was like, *Listen—if something happens and I get fired, can I have a safe place to land?* That was something that I had to think about, and my family asked me, *What are you doing?!* But there's a quote that I really live by in Judaism: "It's not your duty to complete the work, but neither are you free to neglect it." And that was going through my head. I'm never going to finish building a beautiful world where workers are protected and safe, but I can't walk away from this work either.

After 70 percent of workers at Worthington Public Library signed cards to join their union, the library's board declined to voluntarily recognize the union. However, the board did agree to remain neutral in the lead-up to an election. The bravery and organizing prowess of WPLU workers resulted in an even larger margin of victory in their union election a few months later, with 89 percent of workers voting in favor of union representation (Ohio Federation of Teachers, 2021).

Be Ready for the Boss Fight

However, unlike what happened at the Worthington Public Library, very few employers remain neutral during a union drive. Becca, Northwestern University Library Workers Union, SEIU Local 73, shared this story about when her union first went public:

> What brings your colleagues together? One thing that comes to mind is after we went public, but before the election, the provost held a town hall to answer our questions about the union. And we had done enough inoculation about what we call, "the boss fight." So like, what is the university going to do after we go public? Well, they will try and delay. They will say, *Is SEIU the right union?* They will say, *We're all a family. Don't you love your job?* And we made a bingo card with all of these things that we knew would happen, and we passed it out to people to play bingo during the town hall. And that really built solidarity because people used the tools they had and saw it for themselves. Our dean would email the library staff list with FAQs about unions and "your questions answered" and we could tell that they had planted questions for one thing, but also that they were sharing information without studying their sources. And as librarians, we would not teach students to trust this information because we don't know where they got it. And one of my colleagues emailed back the library staff list to say, *Hey, this isn't great information, because we wouldn't trust this. Our students wouldn't trust this. Could you please cite your sources?* And they were kind of caught off guard! Maybe they didn't think that we had thought it through that much. They found out about our campaign before we went public, but they didn't realize how far along we were, how much support we had. It was really great to just see people coming together and sharing the right information, and we won.

As Becca suggests, management typically uses the same playbook, time after time. They may try to slow things down; they will try to *third-party* the union—suggesting that the union is coming in from outside when really the union is you and your coworkers. They will often try to divide workers, highlighting divisions in titles or work duties over the shared problems you face. At Miami University, where Ginny helped form the Faculty Alliance of Miami (AAUP/AFT), management tried to divide workers by arguing that librarians didn't belong in a bargaining unit with other faculty: "In the library, there were a couple of people that I personally thought were 4s. And then when the administration started arguing against our inclusion, that radicalized them. They're like, *Wait, that's wrong.* So that was kind of fun to watch in action. It was truly, truly amazing in some cases, how quickly that switch was flipped from *I don't think we really need it* to *Oh shit, we need this.*" Situations like these demonstrate the union aphorism that "management is the best organizer"—sometimes management's behavior helps workers see the importance of coming together.

In Baltimore County, Maryland, library workers had to get the law changed in order to form a union. This involved speaking out not just to library management but also to state legislators. Bridget, a professional union organizer helping the Baltimore County Public Library (BCPL) workers newly represented by IAMAW Local 4538, shared the following:

> Without the workers, nothing would happen. They have to want it. They have to put themselves out there. *Am I gonna have that target on my back? Am I gonna feel some sort of retaliation?* During this time, BCPL had a director change. Anita, who became the union president, met the new director for the very first time as [she testified] in a hearing in front of the House delegation regarding her working conditions and why she [wanted] a new union. I said to our people [that] I will not blame a single one of these people if they back out because their brand new boss is going to be meeting them. They're going to be tagged as troublemakers from day one. We have to have a plan B in place. And not a single one of them backed out. And I just, I give all props to them. I still get goose pimples on my arm for it. I was just amazed at the work that they did.

Everyone Is a Worker

You may also encounter workers who don't really see themselves as workers, so why would they need a union? It may sound odd, but in libraries we often see this as an outcome of what Fobazi Ettarh (2018) has called "vocational awe," along with the tough job markets we often face. If you have been made to feel like you're lucky just for having a job in the library, it may be hard to admit that there are things you'd like to change. This is a time when close listening and careful agitation will help—even people who feel grateful to work in a library will admit that there are things that could be changed, and you can show that collective power is a way to do that. Fear often shows up in these situations as a hesitation to speak up about problems in a social institution that you also love and respect. Andrea, librarian at the Free Library of Philadelphia, AFSCME District 47, Local 2187, noted: "The only way to fight oppression is to shine a light on it. I think that our society very much teaches us that what's happening in the workplace is private, and we can fix it internally, and you don't want to mess up the facade of your workplace or the organization. But actually, that's what you're trying to do as an organizer. You're trying to mess up that facade and be like, *No, this is what's really happening.*" Silence doesn't serve workers, and it doesn't help us better serve our users. Much as teachers' unions have popularized the slogan "Teacher working conditions are student learning conditions," we know that the working conditions for library workers are also the library environment for our users.

In addition, individualism can be a barrier in organizing. Workers may think that the problems are in some other department, or they may think, *Sure that's a problem for someone, but it isn't my problem.* Becca and her colleagues dealt with this attitude this way: "We thought, well, what unites us? The library. The work we do to help our patrons. And for the most part, I feel like people were pretty supportive. Like *Yes, we should have everyone together.* But there were definitely some people who were like, *Well, the work I do is very different than the work that this person does.* And we had to remind them we all have the same goal of getting information and resources to people." Solidarity means getting people to see that their fates—and their struggles—are connected.

Kendra, librarian at the Institute of Transportation Studies at the University of California (UC), Berkeley, vice president for Unit 17 librarians for UCAFT Local 1474, used the example of remote work agreements to talk about the importance of staying united:

> If people are living out of California, we can easily see management saying, *Well, we'll pay you less than if you're in California,* which degrades the bargaining unit. And then it's like, is it the same work? Having that conversation with library workers is really hard if we aren't disciplined to think about it not as personal—or can't balance our personal situations with talking about class struggle and class solidarity. It just immediately devolves into bad feelings. I don't think it has to. And management wants us to not have these conversations and talk about it openly. . . . But I think that helps us recognize

the situation for what it is rather than just saying we don't want to talk about why we don't have reference librarians, like manned reference desks, at Berkeley anymore, or why some campuses don't have in-person instruction, but other campuses do. I think those are important conversations to have.

Other barriers also get raised in organizing conversations. You'll likely hear hesitation about dues, particularly when salary is a key issue. Workers may feel skeptical of shaving money off their paycheck for a union, especially if they're already feeling pinched. You'll want to find ways to talk about what dues will be used for—like organizing to win a stronger contract and defending workers' rights all the way through arbitration. Workers may have had bad experiences with other unions or have accepted negative representations of unions through the media. They may not immediately see the need for a union or think that, because they like their job, they don't need a union. One of the most baffling things you may encounter is a worker who says they support social justice or even unions—but not this *particular* union. Other workers may support the idea of unions but feel too jaded to believe that change can actually happen or be worth the risk. Workers may also third-party the union, as management does, and you'll need to remind them that the union is all of you together. As Kendra noted, part of the work of organizing is political education, helping workers consider their workplace as a site of struggle and contextualizing the workplace within broader social issues.

We want to be clear: the organizing conversation isn't about convincing every person, or debating them, and certainly not about bullying anyone into going along. Unions are built on the idea that workers coming together can talk through problems in their workplace and often find solutions together. As Ginny and Becca noted earlier in this chapter, sometimes even people who start out strongly anti-union will come around—because management makes the benefits of a union clear or because they see you and your comrades getting things done together through collective power.

What Is Broadly and Deeply Felt and Winnable?

As you speak with your coworkers, you'll ultimately hear many individual complaints. Sometimes these complaints contradict each other—some workers may find that a certain policy is too strict, and others may find it is too lax. Part of organizing is balancing the specifics of what any one person cares about with the broader issues behind it. For example, that policy issue? It may be that the real problem is that the policy is not enforced fairly, that different supervisors interpret it differently, or that there's simply a lack of clarity about the expectations. Often you can connect a specific complaint back to broader shared concerns—such as autonomy, respect, or safety—that most everyone in your workplace can agree on. As you organize, you'll want to listen for issues that are broadly and deeply felt (that is, issues that many people care a lot about) and that are winnable (that is, something you can change through collective action or collective bargaining). Often the issues we care about are broader than just our workplaces (for example, childcare) and we may need to work together to break off a piece that we can really win—at the bargaining table or through other actions.

Just to be clear: the job of the organizer, and of the union, is to address the concerns of workers. Our shared mission is to build power and concretely address big, hairy problems, which requires creative thinking and strategy, but it must be rooted in what workers bring up. At the same time, the union isn't a venue for workers to place an order to address their personal complaints. This is a dynamic system, where the union becomes a mechanism for workers to come together, identify big problems, and work toward concrete solutions.

If You Cannot Form a Union . . .

If you work in a right-to-work state or a state where labor unions are restricted from striking, bargaining a collective agreement, or other substantive actions, organizing can still be a pathway to making change. While you and your coworkers face additional barriers, you can still come together to consider how to address the problems in your workplace. Even if you can't form a union, imagine if every single worker in the library showed up at a board meeting. It is never a waste of time to organize people together, as it reveals why anti-union laws exist in the first place—to attempt to limit the power of workers. You may take inspiration from the Baltimore County Public Library workers who helped change state law so that they could form a union, or from the West Virginia teachers who went on strike—despite laws forbidding it—and still won raises. Think about alternative targets and strategies that would work in your situation.

Also, it is important to get clear on what your rights actually are! You're probably reading this because you have problems *now*, and you can't wait for the long arc of the moral universe to bend toward justice, so to speak. This means you'll need to be resourceful, creative, and bold. The risks will be bigger, but the rewards can still be sweet. You can seek help from local or regional labor organizations, the state labor board, or other sources. Don't hesitate to reach out to other union comrades, because unionists are typically happy to help, and they can always direct you to someone who would know more about your question. Looking to fellow workers in the service industry, Starbucks Workers United has been able to use the process of filing unfair labor practice (ULP) charges to successfully fight the firing of union organizers and the illegal practice of offering benefits and increased wages only to nonunion employees (Iafolla & Purifoy, 2023). Chipotle United has also filed ULPs on behalf of the workers they represent, winning back pay in a settlement after the fast-food retailer illegally closed a store in response to union organizing (National Labor Relations Board Office of Public Affairs, 2023). Your rights as a worker are protected, even if you don't have a union or a contract, and enforcing those rights can lead to big wins.

Finally, just because you can't form a union right now doesn't mean this will always be the case. In Michigan a successful campaign to repeal the state's 2012 right-to-work law generated significant press coverage (Nichols, 2024). In addition to being the first state to reverse such legislation, once the Democratic party secured majorities in the state House and Senate for the first time in forty years, legislators also repealed a number of anti-union provisions that outlawed payroll deduction of union dues for K–12 teachers' unions, froze salaries upon the expiration of a CBA, and prevented certain categories of graduate workers in the state's colleges and universities from organizing (Executive Office of Governor Whitmer, 2023). These achievements were the result of many years of hard work by teachers' unions to roll back anti-union legislation by getting pro-labor candidates on the ballot and in office. It wasn't easy, but ultimately change was possible. Look for people and organizations who are doing the long-term work of changing things in your state and get involved.

If You Have a Union but Want More from It . . .

If you're reading this chapter and you already have a union, but it doesn't do much or it seems like leadership doesn't listen to what workers want, then it sounds like it is time for you to get involved in your union! You'll still want to have organizing conversations. You may find that similar challenges or barriers may come up, but sometimes in surprising ways. You may find that it is union management who is breeding fear or that they themselves have fallen prey to the idea that the status quo is the best we can get. While there can be bad actors in unions, it's also true that sometimes the culture and practices have just shifted in small, lazy ways over years and years—and your union may need your help to recharge. In Chapter 5 you can read about a group of union library workers who helped shift their union to be more democratic, easier to get involved in, and more fun—and it started with conversations with their colleagues. You may also find the description of governance in the next chapter useful as you think about how to build power and strengthen democratic processes within your union.

Action Plan

Ask Yourself

- Think about a time you—or other workers—have succeeded in changing something at work. Choose something concrete: a change to the reference desk schedule, placement of staplers, or something else. How did that change happen?

Readings

Loomis, E. (2020). *A history of America in ten strikes*. The New Press.
Hunt-Hendrix, L., & Taylor, A. (2024). *Solidarity: The past, present, and future of a world-changing idea*. Pantheon Books.

Assignment

With a colleague, look at the *Labor Notes*'s organizing conversation guidelines (www.labornotes.org/sites/default/files/22AnOrganizingConversation_0.pdf). Talk about the steps of an organizing conversation with your colleague. Which steps are you most comfortable with? Which ones make you feel anxious? Where do you think those feelings come from?

Winning a Union

> I could really see the end game happening and it kept getting closer and closer and closer. I'm like, *We're gonna have a seat at the table.* Now, I did have people saying, *Oh, Anita, no, nothing's going to happen, it's not gonna work.* But we kept getting closer and closer, even though we had some little stumbling blocks to get over with the help of our organizers. We only had a handful of people, but it was enough for us to keep it going. And it was something that we knew that we needed to change. And let me tell you, what helps is when issues come up, I'm like, *Okay, write it down, write it down. We've got to talk about this.* This is why we want a union. This is why we need a union. Because we would be able to have a seat at the table to talk to them about this.
>
> —Anita, Baltimore County Public Library, IAMAW Local 4538

While one-on-one conversations are the foundation of organizing, it helps to have an overview of the steps involved in building a new union. In this chapter we talk through the steps of winning a new union. Then we provide an overview of some of the basic things that come after winning recognition for your union. Please note—although this chapter focuses on how to build a new union, you can also use these tactics to rebuild a stagnant union or to pursue changes in your workplace in a right-to-work state. This is a high-level overview, so please check the Action Plan for suggestions for further reading and activities.

Forming an Organizing Committee

Depending on the size of your library, you alone likely cannot talk to every single one of your coworkers, so you will need a team of people to carry out those conversations or to identify who will talk to who. The first step in forming a union at your library is to put together what is often called an *organizing committee*, a group who will make and follow through on a plan to get the union started. Not everyone can or wants to do everything. Some people will feel more passionate than others and might have more time and resources than others. And that's okay! An organizing committee offers you a structure to help get all the hard work done, continuing to build that momentum, gather information, and keep people united as you work toward winning your union. The organizing committee can also help debrief and strategize after organizing conversations—including offering sympathy when something goes awry. If you are reading this book, you have probably at least talked to a handful of coworkers who are thinking about what it would take to change things at your library or who are already ready to form a union. If you have kept these ideas to yourself, now is the time to think about who you might have conversations with to learn more about what they would like to change at work and share how forming a union is the first step to getting there.

A strong organizing committee consists of representatives from each of the different groups of workers at your library. For example, in a public library, you would likely want to have at least one representative from each of the groups of credentialed librarians: youth services, teen services, adult services, tech services, and so on. You would also want to have at least one representative from each of the groups of paraprofessional workers: library assistants, clerks, pages, and so on. As a general rule, the more representative your organizing committee is, the stronger your union will be. The reasoning is simple enough: the more people who are at the table, the more information you will have about what needs to be done to build the kind of library that works for everyone, not just the bosses. Pay particular attention to the group of workers who are the frontline staff. Who are the first people that patrons see when they come into the building? Who do patrons interact with the most? That group tends to have a tremendous amount of power not only in the library but also in the community at large. Though you will want to be as discreet as possible in this initial phase, remember that you cannot organize a union in the shadows.

In addition to selecting a group of people who together represent every group, position, or department at your library, you will ideally want to select *natural leaders* at work. These leaders are not necessarily people who occupy formal positions of leadership or who carry a title. Chelsea, University of Washington Libraries Union SEIU 925, put it this way: "The leaders are the people who showed up and who wanted to do the work." A leader is someone who has followers. A classic way to identify a workplace leader is to notice who new hires naturally gravitate to for information and advice. This person is often not the new worker's supervisor. A leader is someone who people respect and listen to, and, importantly, a leader is someone who, when they ask something of their coworkers, those coworkers follow through. This can be something as simple and seemingly unrelated as an after-work social gathering. Who organizes social gatherings and actually gets people to come? Or who organizes birthday parties for fellow workers and gets coworkers to participate in that planning? Workplace leaders are also excellent at their jobs and are respected by almost everyone. If your organizing committee is unable to recruit these natural workplace leaders, the committee should at least be aware of who they are and have a plan to recruit them to the overall unionization effort.

Once you have a strong organizing committee, set up regular weekly meetings. Having a regularly scheduled meeting on the calendar encourages accountability and can maintain momentum. You might have a standing agenda at these meetings: checking in on ongoing work, celebrating wins, and strategizing about what comes next. Note that the ways your union runs these meetings help form the culture of your union: do you rotate facilitation and notetaking? How do you make time for relationship-building and fun? How do you keep one another accountable for the work that needs to be done? How do you make decisions? While it is important that the organizing committee be as representative and inclusive as possible, remember that it is a group that has to be able to work through conflict and come to decisions, so make sure you choose processes that help you get your work done together.

Finding an Affiliate

Now is also the time to think about which union you would like to work with. Typically when you belong to a union, you belong first and foremost to your *bargaining unit*, which is the group covered by the collective bargaining agreement. You will also often hear people refer to their *union local*, typically followed by a number. Generally, a *local* is a smaller piece of a larger union, and it has its own internal leadership structure. A local may be composed of multiple bargaining units, sometimes across various industries and worksites. However, sometimes a group of workers at a single worksite are their own local. This is often the case in a worksite with many hundreds of employees. At the other end of the spectrum is the *international*. This refers to the highest body of a given union, usually in the form of an executive board and a president. There may also be state or regional affiliations—for example, the American Federation of Teachers is the international union, but it has state-level affiliates as well, which serve the locals in each state. Each of these levels has its own processes, leadership, and role.

This is all to explain that, as you come together to build your union, you'll need to consider affiliating with one of those broader internationals. Why affiliate? Affiliates offer a way for workers to build collective power together at state, national, and international levels. Often, affiliating means access to paid staff time, communication networks, and other resources to help you organize. Once your union is recognized, some portion of member dues will be paid to the affiliates as per capita payments, called *per caps*, to help run their operations, and union locals are often expected to contribute members to help staff committees and activities.

There is no right decision about affiliation, and there is no perfect union. Talk to organizers from the internationals you are considering and talk to other workers whose unions affiliate with those organizations. If you are a public library worker, it might be important to find out what unions represent workers in your municipality. It may be advantageous to join a union that represents workers who have the same employer as you. Beyond your employer, consider what other nearby or regional libraries are unionized and how they're affiliated. It's worth noting that library administrators spend a great deal of their time building networks with other bosses via associations, conferences, informal social networks, and so on. They often coordinate their activities, from addressing book bans to fundraising to managing the workforce. Connecting with their peers is one way that they build and maintain power. You might keep this in mind when thinking about which union you would like to join. If the bosses build formal support networks across different library systems, so should the workers.

Getting to Recognition

> You can't form a union if only half the people want it or even if 60 percent want it. You really need to have a very strong core, but then support across the board, too. Only have a few coworkers interested? Well, that's a losing battle right there.
> —Patricia, Lynnfield Public Library, Massachusetts Library Staff Association, AFT Local 4928

You've talked with your coworkers and learned about their experiences at work, and you've identified what they'd like to change. You've successfully learned who the natural leaders are at work. You've got a team of people who are committed to doing the day-to-day work of organizing, and you meet regularly with this team to share information and plan next steps. The good news is, if you've done all of this and done it well, then you already have a union. But it's time to make it formal and to start making the changes you want to see at your library. It's time to win *recognition* for your union, giving you the legal rights to represent workers in your bargaining unit. Those legal rights are generally confirmed by a state employment relations board or other labor body.

There are multiple roads to union recognition, including an election, voluntary recognition, and strikes. Before choosing any of these routes, you must have already done the work of building a solid majority of union supporters at your library. An *election* requires that a majority of your coworkers vote "yes" for the union—this is an outcome that the employer must accept, like it or not, and is probably the most common pathway to recognition. *Voluntary recognition* is similar in that you show the bosses that you have majority support for the union, evidenced by cards signed by your coworkers, and the employer can choose to recognize the union. (In some states this process of collecting cards, known as a *card check*, may be eligible to be recognized by the certifying body, regardless of what management thinks.) In the case of a *strike*, your strength lies in your ability to successfully stop work until management agrees to recognize the union. This success requires that a super-majority of workers go on strike—withholding their labor and thus going without pay—in order to be recognized.

Chapter 3

In practice, your path to union recognition might look like this: Library workers successfully recruit a majority of their coworkers to the union and ask for voluntary recognition based on that majority support. The library director (or school superintendent, university provost, or whoever the appropriate level of management is) can choose to ignore that majority support and push for an election. Although this seems unfair, it is protected under the law. Note that your employer doesn't have to be a barrier to recognition. For example, in 2020 the University of Michigan Board of Regents implemented a framework to preemptively state that they will voluntarily recognize unions through the card check process (Fitzgerald, 2020). Although this practice isn't widespread, it is a way for the employer to acknowledge that unions are nothing for them to fear.

Between the time you begin gathering signatures on a petition for majority support and conducting a union election, bosses will typically do two things. First, they will attempt to gerrymander the group of workers who have signed cards already. This process is what leads to the final definition of the bargaining unit, and thus those who are eligible to vote and whose positions will be covered by the collective bargaining agreement. Second, they will often launch a "no" campaign against the union or employ common union-busting tactics even while claiming to be neutral. This campaign might feature captive audience meetings, one-on-one meetings with workers, and any number of attempts to sway what is already majority support. Throughout this process, it is important to maintain excitement for the union and continue organizing. If you have already built a strong majority group, you'll be more likely to successfully resist a "no" campaign, and you will win the election. Again, note that state law likely sets some parameters—for example, public employers are typically not allowed to spend public funds on either pro- *or* anti-union campaigns. We discuss tactics for dealing with bad behavior from management in Chapter 7.

Likely, you will come to an election. This is a time when you'll depend on your structure tests—you don't want to go into an election until you're pretty darn certain that you have a strong majority of support. In the lead-up to an election, you might do things like invite colleagues to sign an open letter to management, post a flyer in their workplace, or wear a button or T-shirt on a designated day—all of these are asks you can do that will help you see who will follow through in (often increasingly) public ways. Workers may be nervous about making their support public, but being visible in one's support for one's own union is paramount, as it prevents your employer from portraying the union as an outside entity. Your organizing committee will probably set some targets: can you meet 60, 75, or 90 percent of your anticipated bargaining unit members going public? If so, you're getting ready for an election.

If you choose to have an election, make sure you adhere to any requirements from the certifying body or state law so that your election can't be challenged by the employer—you don't want to leave any room for the employer to drag you through bureaucratic processes. For example, there may be timeline requirements in which you must allow for a certain amount of time between your initial petition to the board and the election itself. Your union affiliate or regional labor council may be able to offer counsel on these issues, and you can seek information from the certifying body itself. It's worth noting that having a transparent process also helps workers—when you win, you want it to be clear to everyone that you won fair and square, so you can move forward in representing workers.

After You Win

You have worked hard to bring your coworkers together, and your union won recognition! It may seem surprising, but organizing doesn't stop once you've won. To continue winning—a strong contract or other battles with the boss—you will need to stay in close contact with members and you'll need to train them to organize one another around new issues, such as the fights to win the contract and then the content of the contract, so they're prepared to help enforce it. We're describing what is called an *organizer model* of a union, one in which *rank-and-file members* (those outside of leadership) make the union run. This is in contrast to a *service model*, in which members come to union staff and leadership with requests to get things done.

Much of this book details the big work that unions do: running campaigns, bargaining a contract, and enforcing that contract. However, we wanted to add a note here about some of the basic tasks you'll need to do to establish your new union to run with transparency and accountability.

Governance

Now that you have unionized, and unless you and your coworkers have decided to form a completely independent union with no affiliate or parent union, you are now part of a large organization and must learn how that organization works and how you and your coworkers might participate in and shape its operations. Though each union operates differently, there are some basic elements of how unions are structured.

Unions typically have a constitution and bylaws that dictate how the organization operates. For some internationals, these documents exist and are maintained at a high level, and individual locals have varying degrees of autonomy in their day-to-day operations. In other cases, you'll need to draft a lot of documentation on your own. This is a good time to lean on your union cousins at other workplaces. Ask to review their documents and identify what will work for you and what you'd like to change. These documents may make for dry reading, but they establish important aspects of how your union will run, both for routine practices (like how decisions are made and by whom) and for extreme circumstances (like how an officer can be recalled). Governing documents outline how power is distributed within your organization, so make thoughtful decisions. Ideally this builds on the existing culture and practices of your union and is a chance to formalize them—such as noting whether decisions are made by consensus or by a straight vote, or employing the terminology you already use—but it can also be an opportunity to build additional structures you may need going forward.

The most basic level of union representative is referred to as a *steward*. Your union may call this position something different, but this person is officially dedicated to representing you and your coworkers on a regular basis. The steward acts as a two-way path, staying in touch with the rank-and-file to share with leadership what is happening on the ground and sharing information from union leadership around issues such as bargaining. The manner in which these positions are filled and the number of stewards at any given worksite can vary, but ideally they're elected democratically by the workers they represent. Consult your union's constitution, the bylaws of your local, or union staff you were in touch with during the organizing campaign. You may want to find out if your union regularly assembles groups of stewards across various units or worksites for meetings, or you may want to start that practice within your library. Some unions provide a stipend for stewards in recognition of the labor they provide.

In addition, many unions have an *executive committee* or *leadership council*. Again, these groups could be called something else, but they consist of officers, which may include the following:

- president
- vice-president
- secretary

- chairs of specific committees or tasks (e.g., grievance, bargaining, social justice)
- constituency-specific officers (e.g., vice-president of tenure track affairs)

The constitution and bylaws should describe the duties of these positions and outline how they are filled. They may also outline how frequently the body meets, how they make decisions, and how they share information with the general membership.

There are some important considerations as you put together this structure. Which body is responsible for which kinds of decisions? Who signs off on the budget? How can your union deal with an unexpected bad actor or dispute? How do you ensure democratic processes and transparency throughout? How are the constitution and bylaws updated? There's no one right way to run your union, but you do want to give your union the tools it needs to be successful. Parker and Gruelle (1999) note the following benchmarks of union democracy: members look to the union as issues arise in the workplace and community; members make decisions about what the union does; members use "we," not "they," when they talk about the union; open discussion informs all decisions; and leaders and rank-and-file members act in alignment (pp. 37–38). Your union may not meet all these expectations all the time, but keep these benchmarks in mind as you do union work. Once you establish formal leadership, it may be appealing to think that the work of organizing is done and now the leaders will take care of things. On the contrary, organizing work must continue consistently to keep a vibrant union running. New employees will need to be asked to join the union, and all union members must be drawn into the work of the union: organizing is ongoing.

Depending on the size of your union and your financial situation, you may be in a position to hire staff. These may be paid organizers, an executive director, a bookkeeper, a specialist in bargaining—you should obviously hire based on what your union needs. Emily, librarian at Portland State University (PSU) and president of PSU-AAUP, described the role of staff this way: "Staff is there to give advice, and sometimes we take it and sometimes we don't. It can be a delicate balance, right? Because the members are the ones who understand the bargaining unit. We understand the institution much better than staff do because they don't work for the institution, they work for the union." If you hire staff, you'll need to be clear on who supervises them (e.g., the president) and other basic managerial issues. To state the obvious, no one organizes their workplace in order to become a boss. Although you may shy away from doing so, it's important to be clear from the start about who is responsible for any difficult situations. (It's also common for union staff to be represented by their own union and to negotiate a contract outlining their working conditions.) In addition to paid staff, you may have access to staff time from your regional or national affiliates.

Your constitution and bylaws will also outline the rate of *dues* for members. This is the money that workers commit from their salary to pay for the work of the union. It is often a percentage of earnings, and ideally you'll be able to work with management to deduct it right from payroll. Dues will pay the salary of any staff, rent for office space if you need it, and T-shirts, posters, and events—all the costs of your union. Notably, dues will also give you savings to pay for things like arbitration, discussed in Chapter 6, or any legal fees.

Members will need to vote on the constitution, bylaws, and other governing documents. Make sure there's a process for revisions, as you'll certainly need to make adjustments and additions over time. If you are in a longstanding union and looking for ways to increase democracy, read over the constitution and bylaws carefully to strategize how to make changes.

Weingarten Rights

One of the major roles that your stewards will play is serving as a union representative for workers in their meetings with the boss. *Weingarten rights*, established through a Supreme Court case, mean that workers can be joined by a union representative in meetings in which they may face disciplinary action. It is important that workers know that they can ask if they're being investigated for possible discipline and can demand union representation. The employer isn't required to let workers know about a possible investigation, but if workers ask, the employer does need to allow a union representative if the meeting could lead to disciplinary action—for example, in a meeting in which a supervisor questions a worker's behavior or performance at work.

So what does a union representative do in this kind of meeting? The union representative can help a worker prepare for the meeting and help them answer questions during the meeting. They can ask clarifying questions of the employer and object if the questioning becomes bullying or leading. The union representative can take notes and remind everyone present about the union grievance process if relevant. Importantly, they are there to support their comrade, which can mean simply being a witness and then being someone to process with afterward. It's important that representatives never make promises they can't keep, and they can't guarantee that the union will win a grievance or that certain remedies will occur. They can and should reiterate what is in the contract. There is more about grievance processes and dealing with the boss in Chapter 7, but workers have Weingarten rights as soon as the union is certified, even before there is a contract.

Conclusion and Takeaways

Starting a union starts with talking with your coworkers—all of them. Through one-on-one conversations, you'll identify the most broadly held and deeply felt issues in your workplace, and you can activate workers to take part in building a union to help address those issues. There are various pathways to getting legal recognition for your new union, but all of them require a strong majority of support from workers. After recognition, your union will need to set up governance and can immediately support workers with Weingarten representation.

Action Plan

Ask Yourself

- What do you think are the issues that are most deeply and widely felt among your coworkers? Have you talked to your fellow workers about these issues?
- Who are the people that you and your fellow workers trust the most at the library? Who will you talk to first about forming a union or rehabilitating your current one? Why will you talk to that person first?

Readings

Bradbury, A., Brenner, M., & Slaughter, J. (2016). *Secrets of a successful organizer*. Labor Notes.

Moreno, A. (2022). United we stand. *American Libraries*, *53*(9/10), 41. https://americanlibrariesmagazine.org/2022/09/01/united-we-stand/

Slaughter, J. (Ed.) (2005). *A troublemaker's handbook 2: How to fight back where you work—and win!* Labor Notes.

Washington State Labor Council. (2013, October 8). *Weingarten rights: Training for shop stewards* [Video]. YouTube. www.youtube.com/watch?v=s8-gmmx9eXI

Assignment

Get together with another coworker who is committed to building the union. Take turns role-playing organizing conversations. Think of specific workers and specific issues as you do it. Then make a plan for talking to a few of these coworkers. Be sure that the ask has been thoroughly discussed and planned by your nascent Organizing Committee and that it fits with a larger plan to win your union.

Find your local and regional union comrades! If you already have a union, consider your state and national affiliates as well as regional labor councils and other labor unions at work in your institution. (For example, at a university campus, there may be multiple unions representing different groups of workers.) Ask to meet or have coffee with someone from these different groups to discuss how you can all work together. It is good to make these relationships before you have an active emergency.

What Makes Library Workers Different?

> As a new librarian, I didn't realize that my life would be constantly advocating and educating for what library workers do and why libraries matter. And it's the same within the union! Even though the union says they will support us, we still have to advocate and explain exactly why particular issues are important to us.
> —Bonnie, school librarian at Fenway High School, Boston Teachers Union, AFT Local 66

Up to this point, we have been speaking about labor organizing in terms broadly applicable to workers in many different industries. Although we have shared examples from library workers throughout the book, you might be wondering what makes library workers different from other workers. This chapter provides an overview of some of the particularities of library workers and library unions. As you read this chapter, however, please keep in mind that having distinctive circumstances doesn't make the library as a workplace particularly unique or special.

Prior to writing this chapter, Kelly was explaining her own union's affiliation to her father. It is dually affiliated, with the Association of American University Professors (AAUP) and with the American Federation of Teachers (AFT). Her dad (a retired public school teacher) was confused: what do librarians or professors have in common with K–12 teachers? Turns out, a lot. Although there are important nuances in every profession and every workplace, overall library workers are overwhelmingly similar to workers in other sectors. We earn wages, we have set hours of work, and we may be full time, part time, or on call. We have a worksite, which may have safety or health concerns. Like workers in industries such as education, hospitality, and social services, many of us work directly with the public. We typically work in bureaucracies of varying sizes, with hierarchical management. We need sick days and vacation time; we need retirement benefits and health insurance. Recognizing our similarities to other workers can be a source of solidarity and power as members of the working class—this is part of why management tries to keep workers divided.

While we wish to underline the similarities of library workers with workers across all fields, this book was written specifically for library workers, and this chapter seeks to address some of the particularities of our field. First, we focus on issues that affect the types of unions and bargaining units that library workers can form and join. This includes how library workers are categorized as employees and differences between public and private sector unions. In addition, as public sector workplaces, libraries exist within specific political and economic contexts. Finally, we address the role of electoral politics specifically as they affect our working lives.

Differences in Classifications and Bargaining Units

As noted earlier, library workers overwhelmingly share interests with workers across many fields. But some of the ways that library workers differ, even from one another, shape how we might organize and run our unions. The different kinds of libraries (public, academic, special, independent, corporate, etc.) are housed within varying institutions or structures that may shape the bargaining unit or even the ability to unionize. For example, at a public library, workers may be part of a much bigger public employees union (for example, Multnomah County Library workers in Oregon are represented by AFSCME Local 88, along with health department, human services, and other county employees), or workers may have a union or bargaining unit made up only of workers in the library system (such as AFSCME Local 15, which represents workers at the Hillsboro [Oregon] Public Library). (In these examples, both locals are part of the larger regional AFSCME Council 75.) There's no one way to shape a bargaining unit, so the bargaining unit is often carefully crafted in order not to be dismissed by the certifying body. This sometimes means that the final bargaining unit may not fully reflect the shared interests of workers, and it can cause tension depending on who gets left out or included.

These varying bargaining units also shape how library-specific issues are handled in contract bargaining and enforcement. These issues may be central to the entire group, or library workers may need to organize internally to ensure that their nonlibrary comrades understand their issues clearly. This could include advocating to have a library worker on the bargaining team or making sure there are library-specific discussions during the development of the bargaining platform.

In addition, job categories or classifications may shape the bargaining unit. These are ways that management assigns work. For example, in a library there may be categories for staff, librarians, and administrators. Individual positions are created within these categories, and the category determines aspects of the position description, duties, wages, required credentials, and so on. It is very common for classified staff or paraprofessionals to be in a separate union from librarians, and there may be other categories that divide workers. While these categories may reflect substantial differences in work duties, this type of classification can also be a tool management uses to make it harder for workers to organize together. For example, many colleges and universities have increasing numbers of "professional faculty" or other categories that may include management and may not share sufficient common interests to cohere into a clear bargaining unit as determined by a certifying body. To give another example, many academic libraries employ student workers, who are very rarely organized. The different categories in a workplace may result in multiple separate unions or bargaining units or some workers being left unrepresented. In contrast, a *wall-to-wall* union or bargaining unit represents all the workers at an organization. This alignment can build solidarity across differences, making it harder for the employer to pit groups of workers against one another.

Library workers also have a variety of reporting structures that may shape how we form a bargaining unit and to whom we direct our demands—who we sit across from at the bargaining table and to whom we deliver grievances. Within many academic libraries, workers are united across campus and bargain with representatives from central human resources or other units. Within a public library, the union may face the director, or workers may bargain with administrators from the county or municipality within which the library system operates. For library workers in K–12 schools, it is unlikely they will bargain directly with the school principal but instead may bargain with leadership at the school-district level. Ultimately our immediate supervisors are often middle managers who lack the authority to bargain directly with the union, although they may be part of a management bargaining team.

The following are a few examples of bargaining unit groups and structures within libraries:

- At the University of California (UC) Berkeley, there are sixteen bargaining units on campus (University of California Berkeley Labor Relations, 2023). Librarians have a separate bargaining unit within the AFT local, which also has a unit made up mostly of lecturers. The union is system-wide, so the contract represents librarians at all UC schools. The union bargains with representatives from the Office of the President, and library administrators may be invited to participate on the management team. Classified staff are represented by the Teamsters, along with many classified staff outside the library.
- At East Lansing Public Library in Michigan, there are two bargaining units at the library—a supervisory and a nonsupervisory unit. Both units are part of UAW Local 2256. Each unit bargains with the director, who may invite representatives from the city's human resources department and legal team. The Library Board of Trustees has the final say on the agreement, though it does not directly participate in bargaining.
- In New York City schools, teacher librarians are represented by the United Federation of Teachers (UFT). Chapters are organized by schools and by function; however, there is no functional chapter for school libraries. Teacher librarians are governed by the teacher contract, which is bargained for the entire city.

In sum, library workers may find themselves in a partially unionized environment or in a workplace with multiple unions or bargaining units.

Public Sector Issues

Broadly speaking, labor law divides workers into two categories: public-sector employees and private-sector employees. If you work in the private sector, your right to form a union and fight for better working conditions is protected by federal law—specifically, the National Labor Relations Act (NLRA). Public-sector workers are excluded from the NLRA and thus need to look to state laws. You might not think of yourself as such, but most library workers—including employees in public libraries, school libraries, and public higher education—are public-sector workers.

State laws that govern public employees may be modeled off the NLRA, but the details vary greatly. Some states have laws permitting collective bargaining by public employees, other states have laws prohibiting it, and still other states have no clear laws, meaning that public employees must organize in a murky legal environment. While there are states with laws that strongly support workers, many laws around labor seek to restrict and limit workers from building power together as a union. Wisconsin offers a useful case study: it was the first state to authorize collective bargaining for public employees in 1958, but legislation passed in 2011 largely gutted public-sector unions. Under this legislation, known as Act 10, public-sector unions are only allowed to bargain wages and to seek raises no larger than the consumer price index. Public employers can no longer collect dues, so unions that depended on paycheck deductions scrambled to find new ways to collect their dues. Bargaining units have to hold annual votes to uphold their certification. Notably, these restrictions do not affect law enforcement or firefighters' unions. All of these restrictions have resulted in the loss of union members and diminished power of the remaining unions (Johnson, 2021).

So-called right-to-work laws exist in many states as well. These laws prohibit unions from collecting fees from nonmembers to support collective bargaining. These *fair share fees* are a way to recognize that the benefits of having a collective bargaining agreement apply to all workers, regardless of their union membership. For public employees across the United States, this type of fee was effectively outlawed by the 2018 Supreme Court decision in *Janus v. AFSCME*, which found the practice unconstitutional. This means that all public-sector unions in the United States operate in a right-to-work environment, even when such laws are repealed at the state level for private-sector unions.

State laws in many parts of the country prohibit public employees from going on strike. A strike, where workers withhold their labor, is one of the most powerful tools a union has. However, even in states where public-sector strikes are illegal, unions can use a credible strike threat to build power. This is when a union has the numbers to potentially disrupt the workplace, and takes repeated, escalating actions just short of striking to demonstrate to the employer that workers are united. These actions could include asking workers to sign a strike pledge, gathering members for an "art build" to make picket signs, holding practice informational pickets, conducting a strike authorization vote, and publicly announcing the results of that vote. While none of these actions constitute an actual strike in which workers follow through on the threat to withhold their labor, sometimes the threat is enough to compel an employer to reach an agreement. It is worth noting that public-sector workers have still organized and in some cases even called strikes despite restrictive state laws. In 2018 West Virginian public teachers went on strike in defiance of state laws prohibiting them from doing so and ultimately won a 5 percent salary increase (Bidgood, 2018).

Workers can also come together to get the law changed. Bridget, a professional union organizer helping the Baltimore County Public Library (BCPL) workers newly represented by IAMAW Local 4538, shared this story:

> At Baltimore County Public Library, we set up a meeting, we started doing some research, and what we realized was that in the state of Maryland, the library systems were created through state statute. While they provide service to the public and are funded through the county budget, they are not actually county employees, and it's my understanding that it's not the same in every state. So the laws that would cover county employees or state employees or even employees in the private sector under the National Labor Relations Act did not apply to these employees. And so while it is your constitutional right to join the union for your freedom of assembly, there was not a process in place for them to do that. So we actually had to have our legal department draft legislation at the state level, because the county executive and the county council were not granted the authority to provide that process. So we had to write the law, get sponsors for the law, and it actually had to pass both the House and the Senate and then the full body in order to go into effect. It mirrored what the county labor code was because obviously they need to fit into that process. And so it went into effect July 1, but, as is with the county, this group can only file for elections during the month of September, which made it very tight, but I'm happy to say they pulled it together and we filed the first day of eligibility and ultimately won our election by 77 percent affirmative vote for unions.

Ultimately state labor laws vary significantly and in some places are actively in flux. Check your local legal situation by consulting the state labor relations board or similar body. State affiliates and regional labor organizations can also help you navigate your current environment.

When Your Boss Is the State (or the City, or the County, or the College, etc.)

Most library workers—public, academic, and K-12—are public-sector employees. As such, the ultimate authority to recognize a union or bargain a contract often rests with elected or appointed boards or with other elected officials in local government. In turn, those elected officials answer to voters. Those same voters may also be patrons at your library—members of the community whose needs you serve. This is a complicated and potentially fraught landscape for organizing and building worker power.

As we discussed in Chapter 2, you'll need to inoculate against apathy and fear as you conduct organizing conversations with your colleagues, and you'll need to be prepared for the boss's response when your organizing campaign goes public. Once you go public, you'll start a new phase—agitating, educating, inoculating, and making asks of the broader community outside your workplace. By this point in your organizing, you've already demonstrated to management that a majority of workers support the union, but sadly that is not always enough to dissuade an employer from engaging in anti-union activity. You must also show the boss that the community supports your right to form a union and bargain a fair contract. Demonstrations of community support might include asking community members to turn out for library board meetings, circulating petitions for the public to sign, crafting social media content to appeal to a broad audience, and speaking to local media outlets.

While the prospect of speaking directly to elected officials and your library's patrons might sound intimidating, keep in mind that members of the community can be important allies in your fight. After all, your working conditions in the library directly affect the quality of services your library can provide. And your community members can help you hold the boss accountable if management is reluctant to recognize your union or bargain in good faith. Therefore, it is both appropriate and advisable for you to speak directly to your community about what is at stake.

Politics

Public-sector unions have frequently been accused by conservatives of political meddling. Essentially the argument is that a union can help elect its own bosses, which could lead to corrupt practices. However, the working conditions of public employees are often directly affected by legislation and electoral politics. This ranges from the basics of public funding or bonds for the libraries, schools, and other institutions we work for to nuances of policies chosen and implemented by elected officials from the school board up through any relevant level of government.

Unions may have their own political committees, which take actions to formally support candidates or legislation, although it's worth noting that this is another area in which to be aware of state or federal legal restrictions. Other unions may participate in politics collectively through a regional labor council or state affiliate. For example, while Kelly's union does not have a local political committee, members have served on the legislative committees for the union's state affiliates, AAUP-Oregon and AFT-Oregon. These committees, made up of union members from across the state, regularly evaluate pending legislation, and locals have the opportunity to vote to support the stance proposed by the committee. In addition, these state affiliates pay lobbyists to work on the legislative agenda established by members. Elected officials also periodically attend regional meetings to share about their work and better understand the issues facing workers. One example of a recent local victory in Oregon was the passing of Senate Bill 551. This law ensures that part-time faculty who work a cumulative 0.5 full-time equivalent (FTE), even if it is at multiple public institutions, are eligible for health insurance. This offers benefits to faculty who would otherwise be ineligible at any of their worksites. Multiple labor organizations across the state helped bring this law to pass. To give an example at the national level, the AFT launched a lawsuit whose settlement ultimately required the Department of Education to fully enact the Public Service Loan Forgiveness program as it was originally intended. These examples demonstrate how unions take action on issues important to their members but not on union-specific issues.

As with all union activities, it is crucial to have democratic processes in place to ensure that political action reflects the will of members. Many unions set up a specific political action fund, taking donations separately from membership dues, which can then be used for approved political activities. It may be possible to set up a separate payroll deduction directly to this type of fund. Unions may sometimes formally endorse a candidate or legislation, or they may simply share information about issues with members. In addition, unions support civic engagement in many ways; by practicing grassroots organizing, members may be more prepared to work on other campaigns, for example. However, clear policies and procedures will ensure that members can understand how political endorsements and other decisions were arrived at and that they reflect the will of the membership.

A union can also help activate members as engaged citizens. Crystal, chair of the Communications Committee at the Boston Public Library (BPL) Professional Staff Association, Massachusetts Library Staff Association, AFT Local 4928, told us about a time when the city council tried to cut nearly a million dollars from the BPL budget:

> The mayor vetoed it right away, and they had to go back to the table and do some negotiating before they came to a final vote on the mayor's counterproposal. Our president of BPL has a good relationship with the mayor, who is very supportive of the library and attends a lot of library functions. So I'm not surprised that she vetoed it, although I'm sure there were other reasons involved—it was a full-scale veto of all of the cuts. But we knew that the city council was gonna go back and talk about what they were going to do. So we sent a thank-you letter to the mayor, and then the Communications Committee put together some talking points and [a] contact list and asked folks on their lunch break to call one city council member and then call another at-large member. The talking points noted that we were very disappointed by the proposed cuts and provided some recent statistics of how our services are used every day and how we're valued by the community and how the cuts would dramatically weaken what we're able to offer. And in the end, the budget cuts did not go through. Whether or not our calls made a difference, it's hard to say, but it was a relatively successful attempt at getting members to get a little bit more engaged.

Note that the phone calls happened on lunch breaks—not while workers were on the clock. Public employees need to be aware of restrictions on political activity at work.

Alan, State University of New York Geneseo Chapter, United University Professions, AFT and New York State United Teachers Local 2190, noted that seeking support for libraries is a place where workers and management are often united:

> Even at the local level, unions can advocate for their institutions, because that's kind of the one area where you're not going to get in trouble, is if you're asking for more funding for your library. That's something management

wants too. And it's really valuable and powerful and a great motivator to have the rank-and-file coming out for funding. There's never a time that's not relevant, and it's something you can get people excited about. And we need to get out of this austerity. We need to be able to hire more people. We need to be able to afford these higher wages. *Will you come to the town hall meeting with us? Will you come meet with this legislator to ask them to fully fund this public institution?* And there have been some very powerful moments there, especially when you have allies to talk with at the legislature. Building those relationships with people who do go to bat for you and giving them the ammunition they need at the state level to fight for you can be really powerful. It's also a whole deal of extra work, almost always on your own time, which makes it that much harder. But if you can get people, or even one or two people who have that bandwidth to do it, it can really address the fundamental issues that are causing all these trickle-down negative effects that we fight over at the bargaining table. It always comes down to politics and funding.

It isn't always about legislation or policy. Library work has become increasingly politicized, putting library workers at risk. Many of the library unionists we spoke to emphasized the political—not partisan—work of libraries. Maty, BPL Professional Staff Association, Massachusetts Library Staff Association AFT Local 4928, shared:

> I think that the conditions in the library reflect the conditions out in our communities. If we see increasing inequity, those pressures show up in our library and on our staff and our resources. At the same time, you have neoliberal pressures coming from the other side—from city administration or from whoever's running your municipality. The sorts of things that they prioritize aren't necessarily our own. That affects everybody. It affects the morale and the work you can do. So many people are very frustrated about this—frustrated about what the institution of the library says and what it actually does. That's not strictly about material working conditions, but it's like the psychic texture of the place. And it affects everything else. There's so much that we have to jettison, especially since after the pandemic. We rely a lot on nostalgia, and that ain't gonna protect us. I mean, look at what's going on in this country. There are forces out there that will be happy to

ban books or to defund a library. It's just so weird to see the library become a nexus for political revenge.

Katie, librarian at the Westland Public Library in Michigan, SEIU 517M, put it this way: "I think that we're impacted by a legacy of political disengagement in our field. This concept of neutrality that we have clung to for a very long time has not served us well. Changing that political disengagement is what it will take to improve working conditions but also improve libraries' ability to function and to continue as a public good."

Building political engagement can also offer opportunities for solidarity. Patricia, Lynnfield Public Library, Massachusetts Library Staff Association, AFT Local 4928, shared about the importance of building relationships across regional labor groups:

> This can be really hard, but try to engage with other organizations or groups before there's a crisis, so you kind of get to know people a little bit and it's not like all of a sudden you're kind of coming out of the woodwork [saying], *Hey you don't know me but I want you to stand up on the steps of the library holding a sign*. It can be really tough because it's hard to find the time or find the way to interact with other groups, which is why, for example, labor councils that are AFL-CIO affiliates can be very important in building community. Again, you're oftentimes not just getting other labor groups, but sometimes community organizations are involved too. So sometimes that can be a way to have a base of allies that are there if you need help. In May, the Danvers Public Library had a drag queen makeup session for teens. Sign up if you want, if you don't want to go, don't sign up. And there were rumors that right-wing groups would be targeting the event. So obviously the LGBTQ community came out in force, but also the Massachusetts Library Staff Association worked with the North Shore Labor Council, which is our local labor council. And they made some really great signs in support of the program and in support of intellectual freedom and LGBTQ rights. And I tell you, there's nothing better than a bunch of electricians and painters and people that you stereotypically might think would be supporting the other side standing with a bunch of librarians and performers and supporting this. Making connections with other organizations is important but can be difficult to do.

Conclusion and Takeaways

In closing this chapter, we want to reiterate again: library workers overwhelmingly share many challenges and interests with other types of workers. However, we hope that reviewing some of the particularities of library workers—the ways our jobs are categorized, issues of public-sector unions, how libraries as institutions are organized, and political considerations—can shed light on strategies and challenges that many library unions will need to address.

Action Plan

Ask Yourself

- What are the shared interests of all workers in your organization? Think across bargaining units and job categories—don't let management categories limit your thinking! What workplace issues cross these lines?
- Library workers are often a small part of a larger bargaining unit, union, or workplace. How can you communicate about your specific issues to your peers?

Reading

Grant, M. (2023, March 16). Conservatives are trying to ban books in your town. Librarians are fighting back. *The New Republic*. https://newrepublic.com/article/170920/conservative-book-bans-libraries-fighting-back

Assignment

Find the website for your relevant labor body, whether that is a state employment relations board or the National Labor Relations Board. How do you file a complaint or register a new organization? What resources does this organization offer for your union?

Power mapping is a way to understand how things get done in a particular community or sector. List the major players in and around your organization: top management, any governing board, the mayor or county commissioner, and any informal but known advisors. Who makes what decisions? Where are opportunities for input or pressure? What relationships do you or your comrades have to these people? You'll want to return to this over time, as individuals and relationships change, but this is a good starting place to think about targets for a campaign.

5

Campaigns

> During our contract campaign, someone put up signs, mostly slipped under people's doors. There's a three-story building that's all glass windows, with a sign up in every single window. It's still up on a lot of them, and every time I walk past it is just that instant feeling that we are strong, this is our campus. It's amazingly morale-building for me as a union activist, and it is like having the faces of everyone who's standing up saying, *I'm a union member*. That really helps with the fear because [with] every person who adds on, it starts to snowball, as people realize, *Oh wow, everyone's in this. I should probably be in this too*.
>
> —Alan, State University of New York Geneseo Chapter,
> United University Professions, AFT and NYSUT Local 2190

As we have discussed so far, by organizing your coworkers, you will likely hear many concerns about your workplace—and hopefully seeds of solutions. But ideas alone don't win changes like better compensation, excellent working conditions, and appropriate participation in library governance. We must build our capacity to act collectively toward a focused goal. In short we must plan and implement campaigns.

Some of the most common types of campaigns are an initial organizing campaign to build a union and a contract campaign to win a strong collective bargaining agreement. In this chapter we also discuss how successful campaigns can create positive change in workplaces and their unions. At its simplest, a campaign involves identifying a goal, making a plan to achieve it, and following through on the plan. This often means synthesizing many individual complaints into a clear demand, getting people on board, and choosing a clear target for your demand.

Chapter 5

In this chapter we go in-depth on some of the campaigns that library unionists shared with us. Although these stories have many particulars in terms of what workers wanted and the specifics of their workplaces, there are important similarities. In each case, a group of workers with common concerns found each other and came together to plan how to make changes. In each case workers were in solidarity, within their workplace and with other workers, finding common cause to support change. And in each case the campaign resulted in a better-organized group, ready to take on future challenges. We end with some overall best practices and strategies to consider as you prepare a campaign.

Democratizing Our Union

Alyssa, Dave, and Althea are librarians at Seattle Central College in Washington, one of several community colleges in a broader system, and members of AFT Local 1789. While they had a longstanding union with a large membership, it was hard to know how to get involved. Leadership meetings were technically open to observers, but the logistics made it difficult to attend; for example, if you didn't email early enough for someone to see your request, you might not get the link to the meeting in time. This wasn't necessarily out of any bad intentions—leaders were busy, and it may have been that leadership was seeking to simplify decision-making or processes. In addition, membership meetings often felt boring, and leaders used shorthand that members didn't understand. Member input in these meetings was limited to polls on minor matters that were unlikely to really shape the decisions made by leaders. Ultimately, as Dave put it, "a lot of the work of our union happened behind closed doors." It was hard for rank-and-file members to get involved—there just weren't clear pathways to take on union work beyond showing up at a rally in a union t-shirt. At first Alyssa found the union intimidating, even mysterious:

> And that was part of my drive to join leadership, because I felt like there needed to be more transparency in decision-making. How can we have collective power if we don't know what's happening and if we don't feel welcome to join? If we don't feel like it's a place for us that we can see ourselves in? I'm also an Asian American, on the younger side, a petite woman. A lot of people don't see me in positions of power, so being on the executive board was very intimidating to me. Also our executive board, in prior cycles, has been very white. I also wanted to fight this idea that you have to be an expert

in order to be in these positions, because how do you become an expert if you don't have a chance to try it out?

But Dave, Alyssa, and Althea weren't alone in wanting change. An informal group of members had started to think about ways their union could work differently. It started in part with reading and learning from other unionists through activities like attending Strike School, an intensive organizing training offered by Jane McAlevey and the Rosa-Luxemburg-Stiftung Foundation, and reading stories from unionist periodical *Labor Notes*. By learning and talking together, members started to identify what they wanted (e.g., more transparency and participation in decision-making) and started working toward those goals.

They started holding rank-and-file meetings, which were open to all members, with an open agenda and breakout groups—"what we thought membership meetings should be like." Members decided to run for leadership positions together as a reform slate. At the same time, a caucus for Black, Indigenous, and people of color (BIPOC) formed within the union to advocate for racial justice issues, including addressing manifestations of white supremacy within the union itself. One of the founders of the caucus had previously been on the executive board of the union but resigned because she found it unworkable. As the rank-and-file members drafted their reform slate, the BIPOC caucus created a pledge that emphasized racial justice, which members of the slate signed onto. Some members of the slate did win, including Alyssa and Althea, and were able to continue pushing from those elected positions.

Althea described three of the positive outcomes of their work this way: 1) "getting the language of 'rank and file' into the collective conversation, like there is a role for members as members in collective work"; 2) open bargaining; and 3) "fun people doing fun things publicly." For example, when Alyssa became communications chair, she made communications more frequent and with a sense of humor, and she brought in the voices of members who were known and respected in their workplaces. Althea said, "That made people feel powerful and smart and included and like there was a sense of possibility and growth and opportunity in the work that they were doing everywhere." Even seemingly small things, like making sure there were snacks at meetings, helped members feel excited to show up and get involved.

Getting open bargaining took time; initially, even their bargaining team was uncertain about allowing rank-and-file members to attend negotiation sessions, and administration pushed back on it hard. When a union uses *open bargaining*, they allow members who are not part of the union's bargaining team to observe negotiations. Allowing members to participate in this way helps make the often fraught process of getting a contract done feel more transparent to the membership at large. As a bonus, members can see and hear how management behaves at the table, which can convince members to take actions in the field (away from the bargaining table). These actions in the field help the union's bargaining team put pressure on the employer to make movement at the table.

To convince union leadership to adopt open bargaining, the rank-and-file caucus held a meeting and invited an organizer from the graduate employee union at the University of Washington to speak about their own open bargaining experiences. After learning more about the benefits of this approach, a group of members decided to hold a rally to demand open bargaining, which they did with partners from other unions. The rally aimed to share the benefits of open bargaining as well as *how* to do it, including tips for attending a bargaining session, in order to "build up confidence in potential future observers," as Althea put it. The rank-and-file meeting and rally, along with the reform slate of candidates and a new chair of negotiations, ultimately led to seeking and obtaining open bargaining. The new chair did not seek ground rules that limited attendance and instead just proceeded with open bargaining. This overlapped with the union just letting faculty into the Zoom room when the union served as host for the Zoom and controlled the process of admitting participants. As Alyssa said, at some point open bargaining just became normal.

If you're not already familiar with how unions build worker power, Althea, Alyssa, and Dave's story of how they fought for and won open bargaining might not seem like a big deal, but it is a very big step toward transparency and democracy in their union. Open bargaining is one of many ways to ensure that rank-and-file members can actively participate in the work of their union, develop the skills to become union leaders themselves, and see firsthand how big wins are achieved. We will talk more about open bargaining in Chapter 6.

Concerned Black Workers of the Free Library of Philadelphia

In the summer of 2020, a group of Black library workers at the Free Library of Philadelphia in Pennsylvania went public with an open letter to their library administration after library leadership moved forward with a plan to return to largely in-person work after a long period of most staff working from home due to the COVID-19 pandemic (Dean, 2020). In their letter, the Concerned Black Workers of the Free Library of Philadelphia asked library leadership to "make good on your public statement that #BlackLivesMatter" in developing reopening plans and addressing discrimination and harassment that Black library workers face on the job. The letter was the result of many months of concerted organizing on the part of a dedicated group of colleagues who wanted to change the culture of their workplace and their union. But change didn't happen immediately. Alexis and Andrea—workers at the Free Library of Philadelphia and members of AFSCME District Council 47, Local 2187—shared their story with us, and as Alexis put it, in the words of one of her mentors, "How do you eat an elephant? One bite at a time."

Inspired by adrienne maree brown's book, *Emergent Strategy*, Andrea described their organizing framework as an "anti-White Supremacy way of facilitating, where you let the energy and the people in the room guide the direction." Andrea explained how this framework came out of their working relationships with one another: "Our core group was stuck together like glue. We were talking and hanging out and texting all day long about who said what and what's going on and have they responded yet. And we were able to do that because not one single person had one job. We were all working together and supporting each other on the projects that we're working on."

Having a high degree of trust in one another allowed organizers to navigate the uncertain times of the pandemic and to identify shared goals:

> I think it's hard for a lot of people not to have structure. I get that. Some people that I really respected at the time were like, *Andrea, what is going on? It's chaos.* And I'm like, *But it's a beautiful chaos, we're all on the same page.* As long as you're fighting for Black liberation at the Free Library of Philadelphia, we got this. That's the goal. People even asked us what our mission was, and we're like, what mission? We're fighting for Black liberation at the Free Library of Philadelphia. That's it. We had a vision, and we worked together to make it happen.

The experiences of the Concerned Black Workers of the Free Library of Philadelphia suggest that traditional union organizing's focus on building majorities won't always look the same in every workplace, and it should not be limited to serving the needs of a demographic majority. Andrea says that "everyone thinks you have to have all these people to do this work. No, you don't." Instead, "you

Chapter 5

need a group of people who are committed, and you need a lot of other people to get out of your way." Echoing adrienne maree brown, Andrea emphasized that "the micro is the macro." A small group with clear aims—in this case, fighting for equity, justice, and dignity in the workplace—can make big changes.

Indeed, Alexis said that the Concerned Black Workers "completely changed the library," despite their core group of activist organizers being a numerically small group. They found the "right people to do the right work" and eventually secured the support of the vast majority of library staff by leveraging their organizers' social capital and talking to everyone they could. As Alexis described it, "Everyone was over this bullshit"—the "bullshit" being a workplace in which experiences of racism and discrimination long went unaddressed. This was true throughout the library. As Alexis noted, "We even had a community organizer who was organizing the Friends of the Library to make sure that our voices were elevated when the Friends went into rooms with library management and administration, and our communities."

That network of solidarity also included other workers. Andrea reminded us, "You're not alone in this workers' struggle. It isn't just libraries. Think about other workers." In fact the Concerned Black Workers' open letter was partly inspired by and modeled after a letter published a few weeks earlier by Black journalists at the *Philadelphia Inquirer*, which highlighted their negative workplace experiences, including allegations of racism and inequitable pay (Tameez, 2020). When Andrea brought together Black workers from the Free Library, she didn't know what would come out of it, but several workers brought up the journalists' letter: "Oh, remember when the *Inquirer* workers wrote this really badass open letter? Why can't we do that? Why can't we be in solidarity with them and be like, 'We're just going to keep going, you know?'" This inspiration led to their own open letter. Andrea noted:

> In turn, [the journalists] were super supportive of us. The paper covered us like no one's business. They were at every event we had, every protest. They were calling us, doing interviews, and they kept us on the front page. So when the Free Library's executive director resigned, it was above the fold on the front page of the *Philadelphia Inquirer*, because we were all kind of working together at this point in time to fight racism in the workplace. I think that's really important for people to think about who else is publicly fighting the same fight that we are and how can we work together and support each other?

Concerned Black Workers took their fight to the library's heavily publicized author events series that summer, which included Pulitzer Prize-winner Colson Whitehead. The author had become aware of the group's concerns and reached out to them. When Concerned Black Workers told Whitehead that library administration was not adequately responding to their open letter, Whitehead canceled his talk as a public gesture of solidarity with the workers. Reflecting on the significance of Whitehead canceling his event, Alexis recounts, "That was the first time we actually heard from a board member who was all of a sudden interested in hearing what our concerns were and meeting us where we were." Ultimately, six authors canceled their events at the Free Library in solidarity, bringing both local and national attention to the library's workers and their demands (Harden, 2020; Schaub, 2020).

While they organized across bargaining units and beyond the boundaries of their union, the protections of a contract shielded the Concerned Black Workers from retaliation. The *Philadelphia Inquirer* described their work as "one of the most visible showings of worker power in Philadelphia in 2020" (Reyes, 2021). Since this campaign, there has been a shift in their union leadership, and whether or not it is linked directly to the efforts of the Concerned Black Workers, Alexis and Andrea both noted that these collective actions changed the tone of the workers across the library—people were now ready to fight, and the fighting was yielding results. Through their organizing, the Concerned Black Workers won a Civil Service Exam preparation training, which could help workers advance their careers and contribute to diversifying the ranks of leadership by providing training to workers who had not previously had access to such on-ramps to leadership.

With the resignation of the Free Library's director roughly a month after their open letter (Peet, 2020) and the nurturing of a strong organizing culture among colleagues, the Concerned Black Workers of the Free Library of Philadelphia truly changed their workplace, starting from their vision of fighting for Black liberation in the library. Alexis summarized their impact with an emphasis on the importance of that vision for bringing fellow workers on board: "If there's an opportunity for people to see a way to a better library, a better workplace, they are automatically engaged and want to get together. People will come together, and they will support you in that vision."

Chapter 5

Westland Public Library

In March 2017 the Westland Public Library, a suburban Detroit public library serving a population of roughly 80,000, fired five librarians involved in organizing a union there. The library director replaced these five full-time workers with part-time employees who were paid much less, citing pressures on the library's budget. However, this excuse quickly unraveled when community members, former library employees, and the five fired library workers repeatedly showed up to library board and city council meetings to point out that the Westland Public Library's budget was guaranteed with a long-term millage. After significant public pressure, the five employees were offered their jobs back, though two of them elected not to return. Quoted in an August 2017 *Library Journal* article after being reinstated, Katie (one of the five who was fired) noted: "I hope that we're able to find a way to tell the story of what happened to the public, to restore trust in the library. And I think to do that we have to be honest about what went on" (Peet, 2017). Sitting down for an interview with us in the summer of 2023, Katie explained that they and their colleagues weren't the first workers the Westland Public Library had fired, and the story of what happened didn't end when three of the five workers returned to their jobs.

In the context of union organizing, the fear of being fired is not uncommon. If we imagine the worst that could happen, getting fired is probably at the top of most people's lists. But Katie described being fired as "a relief." By taking such a drastic action, management provided the ultimate example of inoculation, telling everyone what was at stake without a union. In Katie's words, "The only way our library could get better was by having a union. Sometimes the employer isn't dissuaded by something as banal as the law. But a union makes pushing back possible." Katie gave an account of a chaotic workplace in which management meted out discipline capriciously and described the 2017 mass firing as an apex of many years of dysfunction at the Westland Public Library: "By firing us all at once, they spurred us to action."

Katie remembered the effort to rebuild their team after returning from the firings as "like coming back to ruins. It was post-apocalyptic." Along with their colleagues, Katie worked to build back trust and solidarity through dedicated organizing work, infused with humor and practicality. After a new library director was hired and Katie was elected as the first leader of the newly recognized union, they led the bargaining team during nine months of negotiations, which happened in the same room where Katie and their colleagues were fired in the spring of 2017. The emotional impact of this experience was immense, and the stakes were high: "Bargaining was harder than being fired. Everyone else felt like we won when we got people rehired, but I knew only a contract would protect us."

For many years, workers at the Westland Public Library had clashed with management about what happened to employees and their pay when the library unexpectedly closed due to inclement weather. Sometimes workers would be paid for that time but asked to "make it up" later in a pay period. Other times they wouldn't be compensated for the time during which no one was allowed in the building due to a closure. Going into bargaining, Katie knew this would need to be addressed in the union's first contract. In the end, the union won strong protections to ensure that workers would be paid in the event of unexpected closures.

Now let's fast forward to the spring of 2020. The state of Michigan saw its first confirmed cases of COVID-19 on March 10, 2020, and metro Detroit was a hotspot early in the pandemic. To combat the spread of the virus, on March 16, 2020, Governor Gretchen Whitmer issued an executive order closing "places of public accommodation" by 3:00 p.m. that same day. Under the order, all restaurants, bars, theaters, gyms, casinos, museums, and libraries were suddenly closed through the end of the month. The anticipated duration of the closures was unclear in those early, confusing days of the pandemic when Katie and their coworkers were sent home. That spring, libraries began preparing plans for gradual re-openings and for the provision of "curbside" services, as modifications to the state's executive order were anticipated to allow. However, library buildings remained closed, and services were limited to those that could be delivered online (Mikula, 2020). The executive order that kept library buildings closed was renewed a few times, and plans to re-open businesses and government offices were in flux for months. Libraries—along with other places of public accommodation—finally reopened fully on June 8, 2020.

When Katie and their coworkers were bargaining a contract and trying to ensure that workers would be paid for snow days, they could not have anticipated that a global pandemic would close their library for months. But thanks to the contractual protections they won, the unionized workers of the Westland Public Library were initially placed on paid administrative leave rather than immediately furloughed. They were eventually furloughed on May 10, 2020, but by then employees and the library could take advantage of pandemic unemployment benefits, and workers were able to negotiate the length and conditions of the furlough because they had representation through their union. By winning both their union and a strong contract, the workers of the Westland Public Library ended a cycle of dysfunction in their workplace, ensuring that the library and the people who worked there could withstand exceptional challenges.

Best Practices for Campaigns

These campaigns represent big wins for workers. At Seattle Central College, having rank-and-file meetings ultimately led to major shifts in the culture and norms of their union, including opening up negotiations so all members could observe bargaining. At the Free Library of Philadelphia, civil service exam preparation training broadened career prospects. At the Westland Public Library, fired librarians got their jobs back—and then won a strong contract with additional protections.

All of these campaigns started with some core goal: opening up union activities to the rank-and-file, fighting for Black liberation at the Free Library of Philadelphia, getting jobs back after being fired. Those goals were achieved by identifying and following through on actions that brought people together at each step of the way to build power: running a reform slate in union elections, holding a rally, writing a public letter, showing up at board meetings.

The examples discussed in this chapter illustrate several common themes of successful campaigns. First, the work of a campaign is a group project and cannot be achieved alone. It will take time and effort to achieve your goals, and you will need dedicated partners. It's worth noting that not every person involved in your campaign will fulfill the same role. You might even create opportunities for people outside your workplace or your union to get involved, as appropriate. Among public library unionization campaigns, a common example of this is having patrons publicly express their support for a newly formed union or seeking testimonials from local elected officials. Public support was a big part of the pressure that Westland Public Library workers used to get their jobs back. The Concerned Black Workers of the Free Library of Philadelphia found solidarity with other workers, with library patrons, and with people across their broader communities.

Second, no campaign can succeed without consistent attention to the work of organizing. You and your team will need to have repeated one-on-one conversations with colleagues. You will need to be able to understand the concerns of your colleagues, inoculate against fear and apathy, make specific asks that are in service to achieving your overall goal, assess how your colleagues are responding to those asks, and keep track of all these conversations. At Seattle Central College, comrades were able to make space for members to talk to one another at open rank-and-file meetings, breaking down barriers to active engagement. The Concerned Black Workers were a small group, but they talked to everyone. When we talk with our coworkers, it opens up possible solutions we can find together.

In addition to recruiting a team and making use of organizing skills, many successful campaigns have a third feature—an escalation curve. Your plan for escalation allows you to put increasing pressure on your target as you work to achieve your goal. Implementing your plan can also build skills and confidence among your team as you take greater risks together. Your campaign might start small with a petition, but you can progress to more public actions like bringing a team of activists to a board meeting, staging a protest or march, or talking to the media. In addition to putting pressure on your target, at each stage of your escalation plan you need to assess how much support you have from your colleagues. If you circulated a petition, did you meet your goal of how many colleagues needed to sign it? If you organized a rally ahead of a library board meeting, how many people who said they would attend actually showed up? Navigating your escalation curve successfully will require frequent checks of how well you are meeting your goals. The curve may look natural from the outside, but it takes careful planning to achieve. At Seattle Central College, a low-key group opened up meetings to all members, but ultimately it took a public rally and ongoing pressure from members to open up bargaining.

Finally, it's important to make space for joy amid the hard work of a campaign. In the words of Kendra, librarian at the Institute of Transportation Studies at the University of California (UC), Berkeley, vice president for Unit 17 librarians for UCAFT Local 1474:

> There should always be a fun element. There was a lot of fun during the 2022 graduate student strikes that happened here at the University of California. The librarians at Berkeley did pizza drops. We walked around with huge pizzas, taking them to the picket lines and talking to and feeding grad students. And they were so happy about that. It was fun having these little roving pizza parties. During our last contract campaign, one of our actions was having a picnic. That was it—a picnic! We were handing out flyers, and it was partially to get people out and just hanging out on campus, but it was

also a little bit of a spectacle and fun. Things like that can be little social opportunities to remind you that you're not alone. And that it's not all about the struggle. I mean, everything is about the struggle, but it doesn't have to *all* be about struggle.

All of the campaigns in this chapter created ways for workers to find joy together in the struggle: through a group chat, through snacks at meetings, through inside jokes and humor.

Action Plan

Ask Yourself

- What is the culture of your union or workplace? How do people already gather or connect? Successful campaigns can build on and incorporate what workers enjoy. How would your coworkers respond to a letter-writing party or a picnic in the center of campus?
- Where do you experience joy and connection in your organizing? How can you amplify those moments? How can you weave joy and connection into union activities?

Readings

brown, a. m. (2017). Fractals: The relationship between small and large. In *Emergent Strategy: Shaping Change, Changing Worlds*. AK, Chico, CA.
Fountain, N., et al. (2023, October 4). The flight attendants of CHAOS. *Planet Money* [Radio broadcast]. National Public Radio. www.npr.org/2023/10/04/1197954201/chaos-alaska-airlines-flight-attendants-union-strike

Assignment

Think about what you and your coworkers are trying to achieve. It may be something fairly discrete (e.g., clarifying scheduling practices) or huge and amorphous (e.g., getting sustainable childcare for those who need it). Map out the steps that you think are necessary to getting it done. Can you find any examples of other workers achieving something similar? How did they do it?

Contracts

> Whether or not a union is strong is like the use of a muscle. You have to use it in order for it to be effective. So sitting back and watching other people do things or asking questions of other people instead of finding the answer in the contract yourself—that passivity does not build a stronger union. You need people to be active. You need people to be out there. You need people to read the contract. I can't say that enough or strongly enough. It is crucial, and knowing what your rights are gives you a better place in terms of bargaining, in terms of committee development, all of those things. So you have to use it; you have to use the rights. You have to know the rights you have in order to use them. Just like muscle memory.
>
> —Kristen, Wayne State University, AAUP-AFT Local 6075

Collective bargaining is one of the most powerful tools a union has to make change in the workplace. Through collective bargaining, workers come to an agreement with management about many elements of working conditions, resulting in a contract that is ultimately enforceable through arbitration by a third party. Although arbitration can be an expensive and lengthy process, it offers an external form of enforcement otherwise unavailable to workers. In nonunion workplaces, management can change policies without worker input, restricted only by state and federal legislation. An employer may state that issues like safety, diversity, inclusion, fair compensation, or other issues are important, but workers who raise concerns may find themselves having to seek redress from the offending party. In contrast, a contract or collective bargaining agreement gives workers a clear and enforceable set of expectations for the workplace. Contracts are renegotiated over time, offering the opportunity to seek improvements and respond to changing

Chapter 6

conditions and needs. At its best, bargaining offers a way for all workers to participate in solving the big problems of the workplace.

In this chapter we provide an overview of contracts. We go over broad approaches to bargaining as well as the process itself from developing a platform to ratification. We discuss the roles of the negotiating team and the contract action team and strategies for use at both the bargaining table and for organizing members in the field, the two interdependent arenas in which big wins must be achieved. As we do throughout the book, this chapter highlights ways to achieve a contract through democratic processes, transparency, and active participation. Getting a contract is a lot of work, which can be dispiriting to hear if you and your colleagues have already expended a lot of energy organizing your workplace. As you'll read, however, many of the skills you developed as an organizer will serve you well as you tackle negotiating a contract.

Bargaining Basics

Bargaining in good faith is a requirement. *In good faith* suggests that both parties are making genuine efforts to come to an agreement, and hopefully that is true. However, there are also legal expectations for what this means. For example, if an employer refused to schedule bargaining sessions, the union would have a good argument for filing an *unfair labor practice* (ULP) with the appropriate government body. (We will discuss ULPs in more detail in Chapter 7.) In good faith also means that parties exchanging proposals must work from the last proposal passed. *Regressive bargaining*—in which a party goes back on concepts or elements previously agreed to within bargaining—is illegal.

There are a few big-picture approaches to bargaining. *Oppositional bargaining* is likely what you picture when you think of negotiations: two parties sitting on opposite sides of the table, each group presenting proposals that will be revised and presented by the other group until they can come to an agreement. This approach recognizes that the parties may have opposing interests and will move closer to one another only through compromises.

Less common is *interest-based bargaining* (IBB), which starts from the premise that both parties have shared interests and can work collaboratively to determine solutions. This may look like committees representing both parties working on specific issues to develop proposals together before reaching an agreement. IBB means that proposals are developed collaboratively, rather than being passed back and forth. Emily, a librarian at Portland State University (PSU) and the president of PSU-AAUP, told us about how her union has used IBB since a particularly contentious bargaining campaign led to a strike vote. Although IBB can promote a sense of collaboration with administration, and demonstrate that workers are a reasonable partner in problem-solving, it presents different challenges than oppositional bargaining. For example, because proposals are developed with members from both teams, it can be harder to share the union's wins with members. This can make it harder to organize members. Any negotiation can move slowly, but the amount of process involved in IBB can make it stretch even longer.

Negotiations can also be open or closed. *Open bargaining* means that more than just the negotiating parties can be present. This can be fully open—to the public or anyone who wishes to stop by—or restricted to a limited number of attendees, such as only members of the bargaining unit. *Closed bargaining*, in contrast, is restricted only to the parties at the table. The employer may argue for closed bargaining as a way to protect honesty and authenticity at the negotiation table, but secrecy does not serve the needs of your union members. Beyond the table, these principles of openness can apply to whether proposals are made public (or at least shared with bargaining unit members) or how progress in bargaining is reported to members. Transparency supports democratic unions, and open bargaining, along with full access to all proposals passed, helps members understand the process and prepare them to support the final tentative agreement for ratification, making the contract official. When rank-and-file members do not have access to the full proceedings, including ample opportunities to give input, they may be surprised or upset at the final contract and not support it. This is the last thing that a bargaining team wants—you want the full support of the membership.

It's worth thinking in advance about how to make sure that members are truly integrated into bargaining. We highly encourage you to open up bargaining, but even open bargaining has degrees of accessibility. Althea, librarian at Seattle Central College, AFT Local 1789, talked about the importance of making attendance by Zoom available to workers with disabilities and those with care responsibilities: "When I was working at the women's bookstore in Portland, we got a director who had been a long-time organizer and she was like, *Organizing doesn't happen in paid spaces. It happens at kitchen tables.* And that was a really profound shift for me and I thought about that every time I was cooking dinner while I was listening to our bargaining sessions and participating in our debriefs. This is for people who have jobs. That extend-beyond-the-workplace participation is so difficult if there's no flexibility." In addition, Althea noted that "admin kept pushing for in-person negotiations, which made me feel very suspicious of that being an asset to them rather than to us."

Becca's union, Northwestern University Library Workers Union, SEIU Local 73, got the administration to agree to open bargaining and specifically that workers could attend on their break time. However, it didn't go smoothly: "We had two people come the first time, and administration maybe forgot or overreacted and ended up contacting those people's supervisors to say, *Hey, did you know that so-and-so is at bargaining?* And one person was understandably freaked out and said, *It's good to be there, but I don't think I should come back because they scared me*, and that's what they want. It's not what we wanted. Since then we have had people come to bargaining with no adverse effects. But that is one scare tactic that they use."

In setting expectations around bargaining a first contract, know that this may be an unfamiliar process, and it will be a new way for your coworkers to relate to management. This means building a culture and habits for workers and management alike on how bargaining happens in your workplace—and pushing for that culture to be as open and inclusive as possible.

Decisions about open and closed bargaining, and the overall approach used, may be outlined through ground rules agreed to by both parties. *Ground rules* establish an agreement for how each party will conduct themselves at the table, who can participate or attend, and the logistics of bargaining itself (locations, dates, times, etc.). Often management will ask for ground rules before moving to more substantive bargaining, but you are not required to reach an agreement with management about ground rules before you proceed to bargaining. Sometimes employers will use ground rules to limit workers' participation in bargaining, thereby diluting your ability to use what happens at the table as an organizing tool. For this reason, labor experts Jane McAlevey and Abby Lawlor (2021) say "no ground rules, ever" (p. 34). This is good advice. However, there may be some cases in which engaging in a conversation with your boss about ground rules can be beneficial. For example, securing a commitment from the employer that any time your bargaining team spends at the table and in caucus is "on the clock" can help take the burden off your team of having to do two jobs simultaneously (their day job and securing wins for your workplace). (Note that this provision may also be protected under state law.) But remember, the time you spend talking about ground rules is time you could have spent talking about wages, hours, and working conditions, so don't get too stuck in this particular cul-de-sac.

Preparing to Bargain

Bargaining begins by the union issuing a *demand to bargain*, a written statement to the employer describing what you expect to bargain over (typically reopening a contract before it expires or engaging in impact bargaining in response to specific changes in mandatory subjects that have arisen between contract cycles). While approaches to collective bargaining vary, some of the basics are outlined by labor law. For example, state laws typically outline timelines, such as the period the employer has to respond to a demand to bargain and the minimum period of bargaining before either party can declare an *impasse* (at which point no further progress is being made). In Oregon the Public Employee Collective Bargaining Act (PECBA) outlines this process for declaring an impasse: once the union formally declares its intent to bargain to the employer, the parties are expected to bargain in good faith for at least 150 days. At the end of that time, either party can seek mediation for at least 15 days, and only after a 30-day cooling-off period can the union strike, while the employer can implement their final offer. While the details may vary from state to state, these timelines are important for a union beginning to bargain. You may hit the end of the 150-day minimum but still be making significant progress, and both parties can continue to bargain. On the other hand, effective progress may have stalled much earlier, and you'll be ready to take other action at the end of the minimum period.

The Bargaining Team and Other Roles

The *bargaining team* is the group of members who represent your union in the negotiations. Bargaining your first contract represents a new phase in your union journey. Your skills as an organizer will continue to serve you well, but your bargaining team will also need other skills and strengths. Your bargaining team should represent the overall composition of your bargaining unit. Think about how your workplace is organized—geographically, by job type or duties, or in other ways—and ensure that your team represents those divisions among your membership. For example, if your library system is made up of a main library and several branches, your team should not be composed entirely of employees from the main library. If your membership includes pages, shelvers, assistants, or technicians, try to recruit at least one bargaining team member from each class of employee. If your bargaining unit is limited to librarians, your team should not be composed entirely of one type of librarian, such as public services colleagues. Finally, your team should strive to represent the diversity of your workplace with regard to race, gender, ability, and other categories of identity and experience. This representation should not be achieved through tokenization. Rather, it is meant to bring team members to the table who can represent the authentic experiences of everyone in your workplace.

As you recruit your bargaining team, think about the skills you will need. The ideal bargaining team member loves spreadsheets, is good at math, enjoys research and writing, is a creative problem-solver, can ask good questions and listen carefully, and has an incredible poker face. No one will possess all of these qualities, but as a team you can assemble a dependable crew who will complement one another's strengths and weaknesses. And though you want to pull together a whizbang team, bargaining is a skill we all learn as we do it. The most important quality is that team members be committed to winning a good contract for their comrades.

Your method for selecting a bargaining team will depend on your union's constitution, bylaws, past practices, and culture. It should be clear to all members how the bargaining team was selected and how people can get involved in bargaining if they're interested. Although some unions rely on a volunteer bargaining team, you might consider holding a formal election for your team, allowing all members in good standing to vote. The elections process provides an opportunity for the membership to vest the team with formal responsibility to represent their interests and with the authority to make difficult decisions at the table. Alternatively you may choose to have democratically elected officers appoint members of the bargaining team. No matter how you choose the team, it is important that all bargaining unit members understand how bargaining works and that the bargaining team has been entrusted with bringing back a tentative agreement to ratify. As the bargaining process heats up, having a shared understanding about roles and how decisions are made can help foster and maintain trust among colleagues. This trust is critical because bargaining is a time-consuming and time-sensitive process that requires a significant investment of mental and physical energy. Not every member of your union (even your most committed activists!) will be able to stay laser-focused on the bargaining process and keep the details of every proposal in front of mind.

Individual members will need to trust that the bargaining team will consider the best interests of the membership as a whole, and the bargaining team will need to trust that individual members will bring concerns forward if the team fails to represent the membership. In the end, the work of the bargaining team is ultimately accountable to the membership, as the tentative agreement negotiated by the team does not take effect until it is ratified by the membership.

Each party typically identifies a lead negotiator—these people may be the only ones who speak at the table, or they may act more as the coordinator for how proposals are presented and discussed. Clarify this role within your team at the start, as it will shape your tactics at the table. Because the role of lead negotiator can be a stressful job, you should consider also selecting a team manager to help keep things on track. While your lead negotiator is in charge at the table, your team manager can take on the role of facilitating caucus sessions with members away from the table, and communicating with the employer about logistics for bargaining days (start times, exchanging text of proposals, etc.).

It is not uncommon for your bargaining team to include a member of union staff—either from your local, state or regional federation, or the international—and they have a unique role on your team, as they could be the person with the most experience negotiating contracts. Their guidance on technical questions and strategy can be invaluable. However, they will not know your workplace and your colleagues like you do. Your lived experience of the workplace makes you an expert—although you must also recognize the limits of your team's expertise.

In addition to the bargaining team, there are other ways for members to get involved. Stewards and elected representatives of the union should be a part of communication about bargaining. Each bargaining session offers opportunities for organizing, whether that means encouraging coworkers to show up for the bargaining session or asking them afterward what they thought of the bargaining update. Bargaining can be a slog as it moves on, and members may find it hard to keep track of the nuanced changes in proposals.

In larger bargaining units, the work of the bargaining team may be supported by a *bargaining committee*. While the division of roles between the team and committee will depend on your union's constitution, bylaws, and past practices, generally speaking the committee supports the team but does not sit at the table during negotiations. The committee can assist with the research and development of proposal language and ensure that the team understands the needs and concerns of the membership at large. Importantly, the committee can be larger than the team and have specific areas of focus or expertise. For example, a subset of your bargaining committee might have extensive experience with sick leave and medical benefits and might take the lead on crafting proposal language on these topics.

In addition to your bargaining team and possible bargaining committee, you might form a *contract action team* (CAT). This group should be made up of rank-and-file activists who will support the bargaining team and the bargaining process through organizing and agitation. For example, the bargaining team may need to get a particular message out to members, and the CAT would be ready to implement office visits and messaging and support structure tests along the way. The CAT also supports escalation as strategy demands it. The CAT might coordinate a flyering event or banner drop in front of the administrative offices, for example. The CAT should be aware of the broader community power map (see the Action Plan in Chapter 4) and use that to craft their actions. For example, stakeholders such as library users, students, and political representatives may at various points become important to engage. While the bargaining team will face the employer's team at every session, the CAT works alongside to support the contract campaign in the field among union members and the broader community. For this reason, it is important for the CAT and the bargaining team to work in alignment to make sure that actions in the field reflect the desired results at the table.

What to Bargain For

Developing a *bargaining platform*—the goals you're fighting to win in your contract—is a wonderful opportunity for organizing. The bargaining platform should represent the priorities of the bargaining unit. This means that you must find ways to talk to every single person. This may include some kind of survey, but remember that a survey is often really a tool to follow up with one-on-one conversations. Survey data on its own can be helpful for identifying major priorities (e.g., understanding that 85 percent of members say that childcare is a top priority) and later for use at the table, but in order to come up with good ideas, you need to talk to members. Some ways to do this include the following:

- One-on-one conversations: Stewards can have prompts for one-on-one conversations with members of their constituency; if your bargaining team is formed, these members can also participate in these office or home visits.

- Focus groups or small discussion groups: This can be a way to generate ideas and discussion with members of shared experiences—for example, within a job category or for members with marginalized identities. If you have identity-based caucuses, consider scheduling sessions with each of them.
- Theme-based committees: Once some major issues have been identified, recruit members who care strongly about these issues or who bring useful experience to dig into possible solutions.
- Discussions at general membership meetings: Membership meetings are always a way to raise issues that members care about, but leading up to and during a contract campaign, use these meetings to get ideas, test existing plans, and otherwise share information and have discussion about the platform.
- Voting on the platform: Once priorities have been clearly articulated, have members vote on it. This structure test gives the bargaining team the confidence that the overwhelming majority of members support them as they go into bargaining—or will let leaders know there's more organizing to do.

Whatever combination of methods you use, you want the bargaining team to be confident that it has the support of members as they move forward in drafting and exchanging proposals. Note that the bargaining platform is not a promise of specific contract language. Through negotiations, the bargaining team will make compromises and may discover new ideas for how to implement the priorities identified in the platform. It is important that communication with membership throughout bargaining is precise and accurate.

Your bargaining platform is an opportunity to highlight the main concerns of your members. While issues like salary or benefits are likely to be crucial, there may be other major concerns. Several of the unionists we spoke to shared how the contract can be a tool for racial justice and equity. Christina, a school librarian in the Bronx in the New York City public school system, chapter leader and elected representative in United Federation of Teachers, AFT Local 2, talked with us about the contract as a useful tool despite its limitations. Racism and transphobia exist in the world, and "you can't stop people from having bad ideas on their own time," but you can use the contract to fight against people bringing those things into the workplace to harm others.

Chapter 6

In Amy's last contract negotiations as part of the Thompson Rivers University Faculty Association, two of the union's priorities were indigenization and equity, diversity, and inclusion:

> What's interesting about those two items is that those are ostensibly something that our administration would also say are priorities. But their visions of equity and indigenization generally tend towards a lot of hand-waving and ... even throwing money at things, whereas we want to do more than that. Administration felt that they hadn't had time to consult with their community, and they went on and on about how consulting with your community is so important and they didn't want to accept any of our proposals for that reason. So it was using a principle of equity to deny our actual proposals about equity. And so eventually we said, *Fine, we'll agree to this joint committee as long as all of our proposals can go to this committee immediately, and you have to give us something.* So they gave us two days of cultural leave for Indigenous faculty members as well as the establishment of this committee, and what they wanted was to put in a land acknowledgement in our collective agreement, which is good. I just don't think it actually does much in practice. We also made the equity committee into a joint committee to examine further our equity proposals, which again, we had already consulted with the right people. We went to these committees. We talked to these faculty members, and we put forward these proposals with those [conversations] in mind. And hopefully now that those committees are happening, we can get more proposals like this in the future, but there is a clash about how we think about equity between administration and faculty.

Kendra, librarian at the Institute of Transportation Studies at University of California (UC), Berkeley, vice president for Unit 17 librarians for UCAFT Local 1474, focused on the concrete protections a contract can offer:

> How can we protect people doing racial justice work? What can the contract do to make people feel empowered to actually do the work? A lot of it comes down to what sort of protections we have for people who speak out. Are there procedures or things we can put into the contract to make it easier to hold people accountable? Because on every campus and in every workplace, there's stuff that happens but no one knows about it, because people don't speak out because they don't feel empowered to. They're afraid of retribution. Some of

that is talking to people, saying well, if the union [speaks out], we have legal protections that you as an individual worker don't have. Like if we do it as a union action and there's retaliation, that's a very serious thing, whereas if you do it as an individual, and there's retaliation, you need more evidence and you don't have the same legal protections. Unions and contracts give you a legal framework that has more teeth. It's nice if you have a taskforce to talk about racial justice and libraries. But what's the accountability? Like you have a report and there's no implementation. If you can figure out how to get it into the contract, you know that there's going to be something you can use for the next time. That's been like the big thing as we've looked through the contract: we just don't have all the necessary tools. It's weird thinking of the contract as a tool, but like recognizing it's like if people really want to effect change, how can we help them effect change in a way that there actually has to be some difference or some outcome that's not going to be just another report?

You won't solve all social problems—or even all workplace problems—in a single contract! But as Kendra suggests, think about the contract as a set of tools you can use moving forward. At its best, bargaining is a time when management and workers come together to solve the problems of their workplace, and creative thinking goes a long way toward that.

As you develop the bargaining platform and draft proposal language, it is important to understand what topics are *mandatory subjects* of bargaining and what are *permissive subjects*. Mandatory subjects, like wages and working hours, are topics that the employer must engage with according to labor law. The employer may not like your proposals, but they cannot simply refuse to negotiate on these topics. Permissive subjects include everything else—for example, a union may bring a proposal regarding childcare in the workplace, but the employer is not obliged to engage with that. This distinction matters mostly in terms of strategy and communication with members. With sufficient power, a contract can result in big wins in permissive subjects; however, it is important that members understand the legal context of bargaining. Your union may consider *bargaining for the common good*, which describes negotiating for things that support more than just the members of the bargaining unit, like seeking to limit police presence in the library due to a history of racial profiling. These types of demands often result from deep ties between the workers and the broader community, such as students or families.

In addition to member priorities, research will also help you draft proposals. You may want to review grievance documentation over the previous contract period. Were there recurrent issues that need to be more clearly addressed in the contract? You may also look at language from other union contracts for ideas of how other unions have solved similar problems. State and national affiliates may have databases of contract language you can access, and asking questions through local or regional labor networks can be a great way to see how others have handled situations. In addition, data about your workplace will help you: the salary of bargaining unit members (and administrators), demographics of the bargaining unit, information about dismissals or discipline, finances of the institution, and so on. Many unions build these records over time for many purposes, and bargaining is a great time to look at what you know about your workplace and your bargaining unit. You might submit records requests for pertinent information from management, and they may be required to respond under labor law. However, note that your research may not always persuade management. As Hélène, United Faculty of Florida-University of Florida, put it: "We are coming with data and facts and testimonies, and the other side is like, *Whatever, don't care*. But then if we were not doing that, they would say, *Well, where's your data? Where's your research?*" Even if management ignores or disputes your research, having well-researched proposals makes you better prepared to deal with whatever management sends your way. As Hélène noted, management may ignore your research and come back with a proposal designed around a single person's problem or with a superficial understanding of the real issues, and you need to be prepared to handle that.

A note about contract language: while it is true that the contract is a legal document, it is important that the text be written in the most accessible way. You may find yourself sitting across the table from a lawyer or someone who tries to make the language more formal or obfuscatory than necessary. Remember that the contract serves the union members, and you want to ensure they can read and understand it themselves. The clearer the contract is, the less room for error—accidental or otherwise—in interpretation and enforcement.

At the Bargaining Table

Once you get to the table, bargaining develops a certain rhythm. In oppositional bargaining, one side will present a proposal, perhaps just by reading the entire thing aloud, stopping to explain along the way or at the end. The other side may immediately ask questions or may stop for a *caucus*, a short recess where each team retreats to a private space for discussion. Either side can stop for a caucus at any time. You may limit the caucus to your bargaining team or open it to other union members for discussion. Depending on the length of the bargaining session, you may seek to revise and pass back a proposal within the meeting, or the team may need to meet later to make changes. You may schedule multiple bargaining sessions at a time, which can be particularly helpful when an employer is moving slowly. Evidence of canceled sessions or refusing to schedule sessions can help make the case to the labor board that the employer is illegally refusing to negotiate.

Strategy at the table is both intentional and situational. We may imagine that negotiations are won by brilliant speechifying at the table, but the reality is less spectacular. You will build your arguments over time, reiterating the things that are most important and recognizing where you have to shift. Although bargaining a union contract may feel intimidating, consider what strengths you and your colleagues already bring, such as negotiating with vendors or navigating institutional policies. Throughout bargaining, you'll be shocked that the other side isn't swayed by your great idea or comprehensive data. Being right doesn't mean you'll win. Sometimes the other side will acknowledge that an issue is a real problem but deny that it is their responsibility to do anything about it—especially when it is a permissive subject of bargaining. Though the bargaining team is in control of the action at the table, they may occasionally invite other union members to give testimony on particular issues, which is one way to bring in worker voices and can be especially effective in addressing issues that affect a subset of members (e.g., part-time workers or parents). However, be cautious of letting the employer's team interrogate members who haven't been well prepared. You may find that your colleagues end up making management's arguments unintentionally.

The relationships among your bargaining team members should support your strategy at the table. Agreeing to guidelines for the team before bargaining starts ensures shared understanding and trust before things get heated. How will you make decisions? Who will present proposals and how will you ask questions? Are there expectations for how often someone can miss sessions or meetings? One important guideline is that team members refrain from brainstorming aloud at the table. Brainstorming at the table means you're sharing ideas that the team has not discussed together. Call a caucus instead.

Listening is a big part of negotiations. You'll need to listen to understand the barriers the other side actually has, which sometimes involves asking probing questions, session after session. What is said in bargaining matters, as it establishes the intentions for proposed language as well as justifications and resistance. Understanding the objections of the other team will help you craft proposals that address them, in theory making it easier for the opposition to accept your ideas. This is practically important—to get closer to what your members want—and important for clearly showing responsiveness in your proposals. In addition, understanding the reasoning of the other team will allow you to address inconsistencies, fallacies, and outrageous missteps. To be clear, just because you can identify or deconstruct a ludicrous argument does not mean you'll win contract language, but particularly in open bargaining, it can shift the track being taken.

Taking good notes is important, both for establishing a record during bargaining and for reference in enforcement, particularly if you have to take a grievance to arbitration. Notes document the intent behind contract language. Though your team will strive to craft unambiguous contract language, during enforcement there will inevitably be disagreements with management regarding the interpretation of that language, no matter its clarity. When that happens, comprehensive notes will give you evidence to support your members in asserting their rights.

Bargaining should only happen "at the table." While the lead negotiators may occasionally need to communicate outside of sessions to confirm logistics, it must be clear to all members that these are not substantive conversations. A *sidebar* is a private conversation between a subset of the two parties—typically the lead negotiators—and should be avoided. The employer's team may argue that bargaining would be more productive in private; this means there are things they know are embarrassing that they'd like to discuss away from the workers. As in many cases, the employer may try to divide the bargaining team from the rest of the union, so be wary of this.

You may encounter the practice of *packaging* articles as a bargaining strategy. When a party in negotiations packages articles or contract language together, they are saying, "If you accept X, we'll give you Y." On paper, this can be an attractive form of deal-making. However, in our experiences at the bargaining table, this particular strategy is more often employed by management when they want to exert pressure on workers to accept unfavorable terms. You do not have to accept a package, and the decision to decline package deals should be informed by your overall strategy at the table, your escalation plans, and the needs of your membership as outlined in your bargaining platform.

Though the arguments you make at the table won't necessarily win you everything you want, they are part of how you make your case over time. You will draw on those arguments in the future, when you reopen the contract, and you want to build on it over time. Know that there will be fights you lose throughout bargaining, just as there will be fights you win. Your team should always think about exit strategies for demands you know you can't win—what breadcrumbs can you leave for the next contract reopener? Does leaving something on the table for a few more sessions allow you to walk away with language that really matters for something else? As Hélène explained, "Be patient! What you're asking for in this round of negotiations may not happen, but an idea will start and maybe when it's time to bargain again, it will be easier to work on that particular idea. Take the victories where they are. Sometimes you want *this* and what you get is *that*. Well, that is still better than zero." Elissa, president of the Boston Public Library Employees Union, AFSCME Local 1526, put it this way: "You can't start off your first contract and say, *We want a 30% raise, we want a housing trust, we want this, we want that, we want the other things.* I mean you *could*, but you also have to be realistic. Your first contract is getting a contract and getting some of those basic things in there to start that process. And then you build. We incorporated in the '60s. We're still building."

It can be difficult to communicate debates from long bargaining sessions to members, but it highlights the importance of regular bargaining updates to the bargaining unit. Your team should figure out a rhythm for these communications, such as writing a brief summary email within twenty-four hours of each session and including any proposals exchanged. Although not every member will read every update, it is part of making sure that members are informed along the way. These updates offer opportunities for members to ask questions or raise concerns, and they can be a way to help members understand how the bargaining team's thinking has evolved or where they are hitting barriers with management.

Strategy in the field will occur in conjunction with what is happening at the table. For example, employers commonly hold out on what they consider *financial proposals* or *economic proposals*, meaning anything that may have a significant impact on institutional spending, such as wages and changes to benefits. Use the slowness of the employer to respond in your field campaign. You may draw attention to how many days or sessions it has been since they last brought a proposal, for example. The CAT can say things that the bargaining team may not be able to as they maintain working relations at the table. The CAT can organize members to channel their frustrations—into showing up at bargaining sessions, holding a rally, or other actions—and make sure the frustrations being expressed away from the table match the escalation curve of what is happening at the table.

Wrapping Up Bargaining and What Comes Next

Toward the end of bargaining, timing can become tight. It is not uncommon for final sessions to become marathons, even lasting overnight. The strategy at this point may involve figuring out how many passes on open proposals you have left and calculating what the other side may accept. If caucuses are open to your membership, that space can become stressful as well. During this time, it is critical for your bargaining team and your membership to keep in mind the overall goals of your platform and follow any guidelines you have established for decision-making and disagreement. Emotions will run high at the table and in caucus, as difficult decisions will need to be made, sometimes quickly. The time you have invested in research and in building trust among your team and among your members will help you weather this final phase of bargaining.

All of this leads to the moment when you reach a full tentative agreement with management on every article in the contract. This is the victory you've been working so hard to achieve, and you should savor it. But it's worth preparing for the strange and somewhat unexpected emotions you might feel as you reach the apex of a contract campaign. You've probably spent months following a detailed plan for escalation at the table and in the field. Things have likely reached a crescendo, and then all of a sudden . . . it's over? This can feel disorienting, particularly for your bargaining team, as you've likely been operating with high levels of both stress and excitement. Sometimes you can even feel a little disappointed to be finished arguing at the table, working to turn out colleagues for actions, and spending long hours wrangling spreadsheets. Having confusing feelings at the end of bargaining is normal. It might take a while for the adrenaline (and then later the exhaustion) to wear off so you can feel accomplishment. Feel those feelings. Make time to process your emotions. Plan a party to celebrate your victories. Express gratitude to your colleagues and comrades for their work.

Once you have a tentative agreement, you'll need to ratify the contract. The membership will need to vote its agreement—if the membership votes the contract down, the bargaining team will have to go back to the table. Ratification is yet another opportunity for transparency and democratic processes. If you have engaged in open bargaining and updated members regularly on your progress, there should be no surprises to the membership about what is in the final agreement. Leading up to the vote, supplement this communication with discussion sessions or meetings where the bargaining team can explain the agreement and members can ask questions or express concerns. The worst-case scenario—which sadly is not rare—is that the contract is presented for a vote without the opportunity for members to read it, let alone to understand it. Members absolutely must have the chance to make an informed decision, as this contract will govern their working life for the next few years. Once you have ratified the contract, you can move on to enforcing it, which we will discuss in the following chapter.

In addition to standard reopenings of the contract every few years, your union has the right to *impact bargain* as the opportunity arises. This occurs when there are changes in employer policies covered by the contract or changes in relevant state or local laws. For example, during the start of the COVID-19 pandemic, many unions demanded to bargain over employee policies and the implementation of state laws that affected them. While impact bargaining literally allows the union to bargain over the impact of a new policy, it ideally is a way for the union and the employer to come together to do good thinking before policies are applied. Employers may resist impact bargaining as it takes away their ability to make unilateral changes, so it is important to flex this right.

Conclusion and Takeaways

Bargaining a contract is a huge step for a new union, and renegotiating that contract offers your union a chance to keep building. Thoughtful approaches to bargaining involve many members identifying priorities and keeping everyone informed and agitated throughout the lengthy process. However you form your bargaining team, make sure they have the tools they need to be successful, and continue to hone your strategy and approach until you reach a tentative agreement and ratification.

Chapter 6

Action Plan

Ask Yourself

- What issues are widely and deeply felt among your coworkers? Think about the conversations you've had lately. What issues do you need to learn more about?
- What information do you need to gather to get a great contract? (For example, do you have salary data for your bargaining unit over time? Do you know the organization's budget? Is it larger than management is telling you?)

Readings

Bargaining for the Common Good. (2020). *Concrete examples of bargaining for the common good.* ACRE Action Center on Race & the Economy, Georgetown University Kalmanovitz Initiative for Labor and the Working Poor, and Rutgers School of Management and Labor Relations Center for Innovation in Worker Organization. www.bargainingforthecommongood.org/wp-content/uploads/2021/01/Bargaining-Demands-Memo-Long-12.2020.pdf

Friedman, E. (2023, August 2). Steward's corner: For open bargaining, start early and build. *Labor Notes.* www.labornotes.org/2023/08/open-bargaining-start-early-and-build

McAlevey, J., & Lawlor, A. (2023). *Rules to win by: Power and participation in union negotiations.* Oxford University Press.

Rubin, R., & A. Bobroff. (2019). On the fetishism of bargaining. *The File.* https://web.archive.org/web/20230323032912/https://thefilemag.org/on-the-fetishism-of-bargaining-2/

Schwartz, R. E. (2023). *No contract, no peace: A legal guide to contract campaigns, strikes, and lockouts.* Work Rights Press.

Assignment

If your union already has a contract, read it over. This can be a good activity for a group: have everyone read a few articles and share their summaries with the group. Then discuss. What parts of the contract have been working? What needs to be improved? Is anything missing?

If you don't have a contract yet, find two to three contracts from similar unions. Because so much of labor law is determined at the state level for public employees, make sure at least one is local to you. Many contracts will be posted online, but reaching out to other unionists about them can also be a good excuse to make or strengthen your contacts with other workers. Review these contracts keeping your workplace in mind. What would work for your members? What wouldn't?

Take one of the big issues in your workplace (e.g., childcare access, unfair salary distribution, etc.) and brainstorm ways to address it. Bargaining requires us to be creative in our solutions. Ask unionists at other institutions how they're dealing with these issues.

7

Dealing with the Boss

> I've seen a number of administrations. I've seen good and I've seen bad and I've seen mediocre. The underlying support for members is the union. If you can get your supervisor to go to HR and go to upper administration to work something out, great! You know, knock yourself out. But you can always rely on the union. You can always say, *That's not working out. I've got a union. I'm going to file that grievance.* If it can't be worked out informally, then we've got a union to back you up. That's the most important thing. You're not alone. You know, the person without the union can go to their supervisor and the supervisor says, *Yeah, sure. I'll get back to you. Hold on.* And you're waiting months, months, years, years.
>
> —John, president, Queens Library Guild, Local 1321

Having a union does not mean that you will automatically have democracy in the workplace, or that your bosses will suddenly respect you and your coworkers and view you as equal partners. It is not uncommon to find that management is more willing to raise wages than they are to share even the slightest aspect of power and decision-making at the library. As one library boss recently remarked at the bargaining table, "We don't want to be put in a position of being questioned" (Cancio, 2023).

Who do we mean by "the boss"? This will depend on the reporting structure of your workplace. While every supervisor has a set of expectations and tools to use for their role, for the sake of this chapter we are mostly focused on supervisors who have oversight over the working conditions negotiated in the contract. For example, at a large university, the head of the library cannot independently set working hours or benefits. This type of thing is coordinated centrally in most large workplaces, whether that is through the office of the provost, the school superintendent, the library director, or someone else. Of course, many of the conflicts between workers and their direct supervisors may also need to be addressed by the union, such as how discipline is applied. Remember that throughout all of these relationships, there is a structured antagonism, where the interests of both sides are set up to be in conflict (Dundon et al., 2017). This is key to keep in mind, because you may like your boss on an interpersonal level and still find yourself in conflict with them over how the contract is being applied or because they lack the power and authority to make change happen, despite their "boss" title. From our perspective, being a good boss isn't about being friendly or nice—it is about being fair, enforcing the contract as negotiated, working through conflicts cooperatively, and recognizing the limits of one's power.

In this chapter we discuss how to deal with the boss in the context of your union work. (This isn't about dealing with the boss as an individual worker or in informal circumstances like running into them at the grocery store.) First, we describe how to cultivate (or rehabilitate) a working relationship with management, focusing on communication and structures such as labor-management meetings. Then we discuss contract enforcement, which will likely be one of the most consistent and ongoing aspects of your relationship with management. Finally, we discuss how to deal with bad behavior, including unfair labor practices, retaliation, and other issues.

Building a Healthy Working Relationship with Management

What does an ideal working relationship with the boss look like? Communication is timely and clear, and conflicts are raised and addressed fairly. The contract is followed in good faith, and violations are addressed. Note that a good relationship with management means knowing you will often not agree—about the details of possible grievances, how to interpret specific contract language, or the broader narrative of how the contract came to be. For example, management may claim credit for changes in working conditions that you fought hard for in bargaining.

It is important to note that conflict is an inherent part of this relationship. You cannot avoid conflict and have a healthy relationship with management. This is important, so we'll say it again: you cannot avoid conflict and have a healthy relationship with management. Simply put, working through conflict is how we win improvements to our working conditions. You may come from a conflict-averse culture or family, so facing problems at work may feel intimidating. In addition, you may face workplace expectations to defer to management or to simply "get along," as in the barriers to organizing we discussed in Chapter 2. You may feel afraid of retaliation or of alienating your boss and what that can mean for your day-to-day life at work. However, addressing conflicts allows us to build power and change our workplaces, and it models for our coworkers that collective struggle helps make things better. Given that conflict *will* happen, what matters is preparing with the skills and processes to handle it well. A healthy approach to conflict is not one that seeks to avoid it altogether but rather attempts to resolve conflicts when they emerge through an orderly, standardized, fair, and clear process. In a unionized workplace, the contract often offers a clear set of guidelines governing how to resolve a conflict.

You will probably sometimes find yourself working with management to solve a problem. For example, management may be struggling to get middle managers to apply a new policy, and the union—through grievances or other channels—can help identify specific departments or people who aren't following the rules. Workplace conflicts may reflect confusion, neglect, and misunderstandings more than outright malice on anyone's part. A healthy working relationship between the union and the boss can help resolve issues before they become discipline cases or grievances. Other times you'll be raising problems that management doesn't see as an issue. Occasionally management will try to get the union to care about the problems they care about. It isn't the union's job to manage for management.

It is important that you have clear modes of communication with management. For example, management should know who to address for what—if they send communications to the wrong officer, they should be reminded every time of the correct process. This is important both for your union's internal efficiency and workflows and for transparency and integrity. Official business needs to run through the appropriate channels, not through the personal affinities or relationships of the people involved. This is also true for members—they shouldn't speak on behalf of the union outside the agreed-upon channels.

Backchanneling, or informal communication, will happen, but be cautious of it. Workplaces often have many modes of sharing information, including across workers and management, which helps workers to know something is happening before it is formally announced. Of course, backchanneling may also be a way that management learns of union activities before they're made public. However this occurs in your worksite, never count on backchanneling to make substantive changes. For example, a member may say that they'll put a word in with their buddy in management, but that is no substitute for the change that only comes through collective, not individual, action. Never use backchannels for issues that should be solved through formal meetings. Backchanneling can cause distrust amongst union members, who may have well-justified concerns about how informal backroom dealings hurt workers or go against the union's commitments to democracy and transparency. Never mistake closeness with management for power itself—many a union leader has backchanneled their way into an alliance with the boss that doesn't serve the needs of workers! In addition, friendliness should not be mistaken for effectiveness. An administrator may tell you with a smile that they'll "look into something," but this isn't a guarantee that they will answer your question in a timely manner nor a commitment to take a particular action in the course of a dispute.

Make sure to always take good notes and keep copies of any written communications. You can always send a follow-up email after a meeting to reiterate what you took away from that meeting—it doesn't mean you both agree on the content, but you want to be clear about who said what. These actions will help you with your day-to-day business, and they can be crucial if you come to arbitration or legal action.

Your approach to communication with management will vary based on your preferences, the people involved, and the strategy needed. Chris and Maty from the Boston Public Library Professional Staff Association, Massachusetts Library Staff Association, AFT Local 4928, suggested that the union adjust its level of aggression toward management when appropriate. They said that you should not be at a "level ten of aggression" all the time. In their experience, this detracts from your power and can influence how seriously management takes you. Further, it's important to not lose sight of the other forces acting upon the library in negative ways. Both Chris and Maty suggested that sometimes you might be on the same side as management when it comes to outside forces exerting inappropriate power over the library, such as wealthy donors. The union might have more freedom to confront those bad actors. Patricia, Lynnfield Public Library, Massachusetts Library Staff Association, AFT Local 4928, described communication with management this way: "It doesn't always have to be adversarial. It might need to be, but if you start out going sixty miles an hour, you have no place to go."

Elissa, president of the Boston Public Library Employees Union, AFSCME Local 1526, stated that the union relationship with management can shift over time:

> I've worked with some really good administrators, some really good HR managers over the years, . . . and . . . some really good folks at the office

of labor relations where, you know, we talked all the time to try and settle things or, you know, figure out ways we could resolve issues without going to agreements, and that again that's all built on trust. But I've also worked with plenty of administrators where the answer is *Let me get back to you on that.* I'm still waiting like five years later for some of those *let me get back to you guys on that.* So you never know who's gonna be in charge. And so you may talk to your manager today . . . and maybe your manager leaves halfway through this conversation or halfway through this process. Well and then the next manager comes in and doesn't feel the same way. Well, if that process was started as part of the union, it's not dependent on the one-on-one conversation you had with your manager. It is the organization supporting you to continue it moving forward on a path because it's not dependent on the person on the other side of it; it's often dependent on the job that you're doing or the responsibilities or the expectations.

As Elissa notes, the union can provide long-term support for issues that unfold slowly. Although some workers may prefer to handle issues one on one with their supervisor, there are risks to that approach. You may have to remind members that human resources isn't always going to be on their side. Elissa put it this way: "HR is not there for you. HR is there to protect the organization. I think a lot of people forget that, and I know a lot of HR managers get upset when I say that; they're like, *Well we want to help the employees.* But the organization comes first." This can be a difficult lesson to learn, particularly when employees in human resources are interpersonally friendly and sympathetic.

Labor-management meetings (LMMs) are an important tool not only for getting things done but also for setting the tone of the relationship between the union and management. As the name suggests, these are meetings between the union and management. Each side will be represented by individual members, such as the president, grievance chair, and staff member from the union and the employee-labor relations staff or someone else in human resources from management. Your union may seek to have standing meetings—weekly, monthly, or otherwise—to bring up small issues and check on ongoing issues. Given that putting off meetings and communication is a common stalling tactic from management, having regularly scheduled LMMs is a way to retain some control. Again it is important to take good notes, as these will help you navigate escalations. Consider who has access to these notes or if you'll share summaries or highlights with members—although some issues should be kept confidential for individual privacy, you will want to find ways to be transparent with members about what happens in these meetings.

What you can achieve with LMMs may vary. In fact a common tactic used by bosses to attack workers' self-organization through unions is to attempt to seriously limit the opportunities for workers to negotiate conditions in the workplace. For example, management might decide, unilaterally, that they "can't" discuss working conditions outside of contract bargaining and will claim that their hands are tied on issues such as reclassification or rule-making "because of the union." This is false. What they are really saying is that they refuse to engage with your union outside of the limited window of contract bargaining because they know that engaging with your union creates an expectation that such an engagement might lead to an agreement or a negotiated understanding about something related to the workplace.

In addition to standing meetings, you may have occasional labor-management committees or working groups. These may be mandated by your collective bargaining agreement, for example, to investigate a problem that was not resolved by the contract and make recommendations. Often these work to set the stage for future contract negotiations by outlining the issue and proposed solutions. Note that the success of these taskforces will vary: while ideally they bring together representatives from both sides who are committed to making change, some of the participants may have other goals. For your union, this can be a great opportunity to activate members with a passion about the specific topic at hand.

Contract Enforcement

In the previous chapter, we described the process of bargaining and ratifying a collective bargaining agreement. Once you have a contract, the next step is making sure that it is thoroughly and fairly implemented. Contract enforcement will then become one of the primary areas of your union's relationship with management.

Many parts of contract enforcement will be straightforward. For example, you may have incorporated existing workplace policy into the contract, which hopefully is already being applied. Ideally wage increases can be applied through existing tools. In other cases, you may have totally new structures or practices to implement, or there may be issues that the union has agreed to continue working on with the employer in a labor-management committee. In the case of these newer elements, your union will have additional work to do to ensure that all members of your bargaining unit understand what the contract means for their working conditions and to encourage people to come to their union when they have concerns. Know that some things will invariably go wrong in enforcing the contract, whether through malice, neglect, or pure misunderstanding.

With a new contract, consider how you'll make sure that members understand it. If you had a transparent and democratic process for ratifying the contract, this work has already begun: members should have an understanding of the big picture of the contract and have had time to review the language before they voted. However, contracts are typically long and complex documents, and ongoing education is necessary. After ratification, consider how to ensure that activists—including elected officers, stewards, and so on—have a strong overview of the contract, such as through a contract reading "book club" or other opportunities to study the material in depth. You can introduce an aspect of the contract at each monthly meeting, or schedule contract enforcement trainings for new leaders. When active members are organizing, they need to listen for issues that may be possible contract violations. As discussed in Chapter 2, an organizing conversation means listening closely for concerns and being prepared to dig deeper. Rank-and-file workers may have a sense of the contract's protections overall but not realize that their issue represents a violation. On the other hand, workers may have an inflated sense of what the union can do for them and seek redress for something not covered in the contract.

Many unions will keep track of issues in some way, whether they rise to the level of grievances or not. This is particularly important with a large bargaining unit and for noticing patterns over time. If you have been keeping records for an organizing campaign, this will give you a good starting place. While the details will need to match your union's culture and capacity, what is important is that union activists can recognize when an issue needs to be passed along to ensure it gets addressed.

A *grievance* is the way that the union seeks to correct and address contract violations. Your contract likely outlines the specific process for grievances, such as who is responsible for various duties along the way, but we'll overview the general idea here. Unions typically have a grievance officer, who may work with a broader committee, to support members grieving contract violations. Members of the bargaining team may transition well into the work of enforcement, as they bring deep knowledge of the contract.

A grievance starts when a potential violation of the contract is identified. A member may come to the union with a concern, or a union activist may uncover an issue during an organizing conversation. In some cases, the employer may share some communication that sparks a grievance due to how they're describing or implementing activities outlined in the contract. Depending on the situation, the grievance officer will talk to the workers involved to get more information. Dates are very important in pursuing grievances, as there may be limitations within your contract on how long after the alleged violation a grievance can be filed, so it is important to encourage workers to speak up as soon as possible with their concerns.

Patricia, Lynnfield Public Library, Massachusetts Library Staff Association, AFT Local 4928, noted that identifying grievances is a great way to engage members:

> It is also super important to educate the membership about what is a grievance and what isn't. Your manager not saying *hi* to you in the hall is not a grievance. And it's exhausting for a chapter chair if they're constantly being bombarded by nongrievances, nonactionable things. So I think it's important, and another good way to engage membership is by putting some of the onus on them. Okay, you think this is a grievance? Tell me how. Show me in the contract. What do you think we should do? And so, not always having people come to you for the answers like, *This happened to me, do something.* They've got to be part of the process. It's not just top-down where someone up here takes care of everything. It's very collective. I mean, it's collective bargaining, collective actions. And that will engage membership, by coming out from that perspective.

Your grievance committee should have a clear process for deciding to proceed with a grievance at each step and a process for informing other leadership. Because grievances can, if pursued to arbitration, become incredibly expensive, it is important to have processes that ensure that each step is taken with the best interest of the union and its members.

The most common types of grievances will be the union representing a worker (or a group of workers) and the union grieving on its own behalf. The union grieves on its own behalf for things related to union-employer relations. For example, if the contract outlines how employee lists are to be shared and updated, and the employer does not follow through, the union may grieve that violation on its own behalf. It's important to note that grievances are filed against the employer rather than any particular actor. For example, if your contract protects workers from harassment at work, and they have an ongoing issue with a coworker—even one in the same bargaining unit—the grievance will be against the employer for not ensuring a safe workplace for that worker.

The process is often described in terms of steps one, two, and three—the specifics of each step will likely be described in your contract, but the following are common general processes, which escalate over time. Not all workplaces will have three steps. Smaller workplaces generally have fewer steps.

In step one, the grievance is formally filed, typically in a written format, outlining which clauses of the contract appear to be violated and providing justification. In addition, the written grievance will outline proposed remedies. For example, if a worker is being denied due process in a disciplinary matter, the remedy may include that due process be implemented and any existing discipline be removed, including from any personnel files. This written grievance is submitted to the employer, typically a particular person or office—step one may start with the department manager, for example. This person may be required to meet with the grievant and then will have a set period of time in which to make a response, typically in writing. If the grievant is not satisfied with that response, they can appeal in step two, which goes to a higher level, and perhaps a third step.

If the grievant isn't satisfied with the response at the highest level, the grievance can be moved into arbitration. Specific details of this process are likely outlined in your contract, but the overall picture should be similar. You may be required to work with a mediator prior to moving forward with arbitration, but at the point of seeking arbitration, you will need to identify an arbitrator, and you'll have a process outlined in your contract with the employer for mutually selecting one. The arbitrator will schedule a hearing to receive the position and evidence presented by each party, and then offer a decision. These decisions are binding. Your contract likely outlines how you'll pay the arbitrator's fees—it may be that the losing party pays the entire fee or costs are split between parties.

Arbitration is a powerful tool for enforcing the contract: while the grievance process is otherwise internal, where the employer evaluates their own actions, arbitration brings in a third party to evaluate a potential violation. Because the decision of an arbitration is binding, it may require the employer to adhere to a remedy that is costly or that shifts workplace activities in a way they do not like. However, arbitration can also be slow and costly—a worker affected by a serious grievance may have quit their job and moved on before the arbitration gets settled. Then there may be decisions that support the employer, of course. Thus, the threat of arbitration is at the far end of all contract enforcement.

Chapter 7

Dealing with Bad Behavior

Bad behaviors from management can come in many forms. There may be individual acts by individual bosses, such as hassling workers for their union activities or for other reasons. In addition, management may act in more coordinated ways to limit the power of workers, including in ways that infringe on legally protected rights.

Retaliation is a common fear of potential union members in a tense workplace. The National Labor Relations Act protects workers against retaliation for organizing and union activity; many state laws protect the rights of public employees for this as well. Ironically workers who are the most visible in their union support are often best protected by this visibility—it would make a retaliation case more clearcut. However, in addition to outright retaliation, unionists may face more subtle forms of intimidation due to their union activities. This is particularly difficult in a toxic workplace or where bullying occurs regardless of union activities.

Kristen, Wayne State University AAUP-AFT Local 6075, had this to say about retaliation:

> The more active you are, the more protection you have. The more public your activity, the more out there you are with respect to your union work, then you have protection from anti-union discrimination. You have a potential unfair labor practice; there are a lot of different tools that can be utilized to combat an administrator or set of administrators or a hostile administration in general from coming after you for being union-forward and protecting your fellow coworkers. There is protection in that, and that's something that I try to drive home with the academic staff that I represent because that fear is strong. There is almost this ingrained belief when you first start [a job] that you have to keep your head down. You can't make any noise. You can't do anything that's too controversial, and oh my God, stay away from the union. So when new people start, we have this council rep system that is like our version of a steward system. So we have council reps for departments, for colleges, and as soon as somebody starts, we're on them right away. Like, *Have you signed the slip yet? Have you submitted your dues deduction form? This is why you need to do that.* We give them concrete examples of things that have happened in their area, and then they know, *Oh, okay, these people are here to help me, not to make my life more difficult.* Which is something

that administrators often say, *You don't wanna be involved with the union. It's just gonna be too complicated. It's gonna be too difficult. They're gonna draw you into things; they're gonna get you in trouble.* So we try to counteract that right from the get-go.

In general, whether retaliation is clear-cut or harder to prove, acts of intimidation from the boss depend on the fear and isolation of workers. As Kristen described, it is crucial that everyone understands that the union has their back. Encourage members to speak to their steward when they experience bad behavior from a boss. It may rise to the level of a formal grievance, but even recognizing patterns and brainstorming tactics together can help. When there is one rogue bad manager, central administration may have their own interest in reining that person in. This is an area where LMMs can be productive.

Beyond grievances, there are other tools you can use to address bad behavior. An *unfair labor practice* (ULP), which Kristen mentioned, describes activities that violate state or national labor laws. Typically, you'll file a ULP with the appropriate labor board, such as at the state level. Filing a ULP may have some costs, like legal fees, but it is likely to be less expensive (and faster) than taking a grievance to arbitration. In addition, ULP rulings may set precedence for standards in the jurisdiction. This raises the stakes for the employer—if they adamantly want to continue their behavior, they're likely to fight the ULP. While you absolutely should file ULPs, it is important to note that they are a limited tool. Because of its timeline, the issue at hand may be moot by the time the ruling occurs—for example, if there's a ULP occurring during a unionization campaign, your election date may be long gone by the time the ULP is resolved. In addition, while the ruling may require the employer to stop that behavior now, that may not stop them from trying something similar in the future. Filing a ULP has limits as an enforcement mechanism, as it can only chase after bad behavior, not prevent it. ULPs are a tool alongside others, such as grievances, which you'll likely use more rigorously.

Conclusion and Takeaways

A healthy relationship with management will serve you and your comrades well. This doesn't mean you have to be buddy-buddy (or constantly angry) with your boss. Instead it means building processes and skills to deal with conflict as it arises. The grievance process will help you enforce your contract, and your union also has tools to address bad behavior.

Chapter 7

Action Plan

Ask Yourself

- What fears do you have about confronting management? The better you can name and address your own concerns, the more prepared you'll be to advocate for yourself and your colleagues. Think of this as inoculating yourself. Consider your personal approach to conflict as well as norms in your workplace. What will you need to change to more functionally address problems?
- What practices are currently in place in your union for labor management meetings and other regular communications with management? If you don't know, ask your steward or leadership. How do (or don't) these practices reflect the values of transparency and democracy?

Readings

Last Week Tonight with John Oliver. (2021, November 14). *Union busting* [Video]. YouTube. www.youtube.com/watch?v=Gk8dUXRpoy8

Singh, S. (2016, January 6). How to beat retaliation, even without a union. *Labor Notes.* www.labornotes.org/2016/01/how-beat-retaliation-even-without-union

Assignment

Step one in the grievance process is typically a meeting with a supervisor. Role play this kind of meeting using a common violation of your own contract. If you don't have a contract yet, role play how you'd support someone in a potential disciplinary meeting. Even if you don't have a union yet, building skills for staying calm and clear in a fraught circumstance will help you!

Elissa, president of the Boston Public Library Employees Union, AFSCME Local 1526, suggests asking to attend a grievance or arbitration hearing. You may need to ask around in other unions to see if you can find an active hearing, and of course, it should be with the consent of the affected member.

Our Vision for the Future

> There's this beautiful thing of solidarity that I never truly understood until I started organizing. And what that meant, to really have people have your back. You know, I'm thankful for my employer. I am thankful for my job. But at the end of the day, I'm an employee. We are not all family here. And having solidarity with other library workers, going to [the American Library Association's conference] for the first time this past year and seeing sessions about unionizing? I almost cried. It was so beautiful to see and to have things like this, getting together and sharing stories. And I really hope that future librarians who see this . . . see it can be done, it has been done, and you have people who want to help. Remember why you started wanting to work in libraries. Don't give up. It's not gonna be easy, but don't give up, because at the end of the day, you can have this beautiful workplace where you still work in your library, [and] you have better working conditions. You're valued and you're validated at work. Two years ago I almost quit, and I'm so glad that I didn't.
>
> —Tara, vice president, Worthington Public Libraries United, Ohio Federation of Teachers Local 6606

We are completing this book during an exciting moment in the history of the American labor movement. Decades of attacks on working people, the gutting of public funding for public institutions, and the erosion of trust in public institutions and the people who run them have led to a steady decline in union participation. According to the US Bureau of Labor Statistics (2024), 2022 marked the lowest numbers since the agency began gathering such data in 1983 with just 10.1 percent of American workers belonging to a union.

These numbers stand in contrast to what those of us who are active in the labor movement see and hear on the ground. It isn't just the high-profile organizing campaigns in Starbucks, Amazon, and other corporate settings but the push for unions in libraries in particular that give us hope. The stories in these pages document those efforts, marking first locals and first contracts alongside the everyday advantages of organized libraries: higher wages, greater autonomy, and a place at the table when decisions about wages and working conditions are made.

So what comes next? First, we need to build on the victories we've notched over the past several years. That means celebrating wins—every single one of them, no matter how small—and making sure that everyone knows that when we fight we win. This book is one contribution to that project.

Second, we need to make the case that library worker unions contribute to better library services for the community. Workers who are compensated fairly and enjoy agency in their workplaces are better workers. Ensuring that organizing demands include elements like safe staffing ratios in public and school libraries is one way to increase support for public-sector unions. More library workers means the library can offer more programming, more access to resources, and more safety. Adding public-sector workers strengthens public institutions. Unions are a key tool for expanding the workforce.

We also need to tie labor organizing to other kinds of organizing work for a better world. We can't see library workforce issues in isolation from the rest of the world. Although this volume is written for library workers who want to organize, the lessons are applicable to any kind of organizing. Shaping demands, selecting targets, building collective power conversation by conversation—these are all relevant to forming a union, advocating for policies that reject attempts to ban and censor materials, and any other effort to make material change that we might engage in—even something as simple as making the case for a new coffee machine in the break room.

We must also recognize that the terrain on which we struggle is not determined entirely by the boss or the boards of trustees. Take the credible strike threat, for example. This is a crucial tool for wielding worker power. When we withhold our labor, it becomes clear to everyone that the institution only works if and when we do. Building the power necessary to go on strike is at the heart of union work, the ultimate goal of any organizing drive. The strategies we discuss in this volume—one-on-one conversations, assessments, structure tests—contribute to that goal. Many social, political, and economic factors work against us. For example, tying health insurance coverage to employment drastically increases the stakes of a strike action. Withholding our labor can mean risking not just our livelihoods but our very lives. The Taylor Act, passed in New York in 1967, prohibits public-sector workers from striking. A lack of affordable childcare constrains the time working parents have to organize outside of work hours. Racism, patriarchy, and xenophobia put solidarity at risk. We must contend with the systems and structures that limit our capacity to build worker power.

For some of us, this will mean engaging with electoral politics at local, state, and national levels. We saw the difference this can make when President Joe Biden appointed pro-labor attorney Jennifer Abruzzo as general counsel of the National Labor Relations Board in 2021. This appointment led to a series of rulings that made it easier to gain recognition for graduate employee union locals. Legalizing public-sector strikes in New York will also require legislative action. For others of us, this will mean engaging with social movements beyond the ballot box. Struggles for racial justice are also struggles for worker solidarity. Organizing for a socialist future also means organizing for a world where worker power is an essential component of the social and economic infrastructure. Social and political movements shape the terrain of struggle and require our engagement.

What you won't find in our vision for the future is the answer to the question that animates all of us who wish for a better, more equitable world: what is to be done? There is no correct answer to this question. One thing we learn in the struggle is that it is impossible to know in advance what will get the win. Did Oregon State University faculty get a union because Kelly made just one more phone call? Did the lockout at Long Island University, Brooklyn end because Emily bought a louder bullhorn? Did librarians at the University of Michigan form a union because Meredith saw Jane McAlevey speak? Did East Lansing Public Library staff unionize on the strength of Angelo's arguments? All of these activities surely contributed to the labor movement in libraries, but none are sufficient in themselves to win the world we want. What's most important is that everyone does something. Maybe that's joining with colleagues to power map your workplace. Maybe that's talking with a colleague who is on the fence about unions. Maybe that means ordering buttons for everyone in the library to wear. Every time we take a concrete action to bring people together, we contribute to building collective power. It's more important to do something than to do the right thing. And when we act together, we also build a shared analysis, rooted in the material struggle, that can push us in the right direction. But we must act in order to get there.

Chapter 8

Action Plan
Ask Yourself

- Thinking beyond your workplace, what else do you want to see change in your community and the broader world? Are any of these concerns shared by your coworkers?

Reading

McAlevey, J. (2020). As go unions, so goes the republic. In *A collective bargain: Unions, organizing, and the fight for democracy*. Ecco.

Assignment

Think about some of the big issues beyond your workplace. Where do you have existing (or potential) relationships and connections? Who shares your concerns? Who makes decisions in this sphere? Create a visual representation of the power networks in your broader community, thinking of some of the big issues beyond your workplace. Keep this in a place you can refer back to often.

Bonus: If You're Reading This and You're the Boss

When library workers kick off union organizing efforts in their workplaces or robustly use tools like the grievance process to enforce the contract, managers can get defensive. *Why is my staff unionizing when I'm a pretty good boss? Why did they file a grievance when I am doing my best!* In this chapter we discuss the relationship between supervisors and managers and the unionized (and unionizing!) library workers who have so far been the focus of this book. Taken together, legal changes such as the Taft-Hartley Act in 1947 and more recently the Supreme Court ruling in *Janus v. AFSCME* in 2018, outlined in Chapters 2 and 4, have produced a decline in union density. And when fewer people are members of unions, fewer people know what unions do, how they operate, and the contribution a union can make to the quality of life for working people. So if unions are new to you, you're in good company, and that's by design.

Our intention here is to depersonalize the relationship between management and labor in the context of a union contract. We know it can be challenging to hear that people who are colleagues one day are organizing the next, and it's easy to take that personally. But unions are structural support for everyone at work, not just the people represented by the bargaining unit. We believe that managers who understand and value the collective bargaining agreement and see what it contributes to the workplace can better support the union efforts of the workers who organize them. Rather than depending on good bosses who care about employees and want to do right by them, a union mandates those things. For example, the grievance process includes a set of rules that must be followed, from the format of the paperwork to steps and deadlines that ensure all parties move forward. Complaints about salary, fringe benefits, and responsibilities and accountabilities are defined in the contract with clear indicators of when problems are resolved. In a nonunion workplace, complaints can drag on and on with no clear mechanism for their resolution. In union workplaces, all parts of the process are defined. As long as both parties agree to the process, they can abide by the conclusion.

Union Myth-Busting

My Staff Is Against Me

When you think *union* you may picture crowds of angry, sign-wielding protesters screaming about how much they hate the boss. However, although organized labor certainly can mean protest, it doesn't have to, and, crucially, it doesn't always. Conflict between management and staff is normal, whether you have a union in the workplace or not—any time there's a difference in power between two parties, expect some friction! We can all think of examples where managers and staff work together effectively toward shared goals and plenty where they don't, probably in the very same institution! It doesn't take a union to produce conflict in the workplace. Unions *structure* antagonism; they don't *produce* it.

And while we're talking about the boss: if you have a boss, you're not the boss! Wages and working conditions—the bread and butter of union work—are probably not something you can determine on your own. Supervisors, middle managers, coordinators, and all the job titles we use to indicate who is in charge of certain people and projects, don't usually have control over how much money a person makes, the vacation time they get, or what workplace safety looks like. If you're in one of these positions, it's very likely that you'll be expected to enforce rules that come down from the actual boss rather than making them on your own. When library workers organize, they're pressuring the boss-boss, the person in the workplace hierarchy who has the final say when it comes to what work looks like. Unless you're the chancellor, director, superintendent, or president, you're not the target.

You are also not responsible for the terrible things the boss-boss might do. When we're working as a supervisor or middle manager, it can be easy to fall into the trap of thinking we can protect our colleagues from mismanagement at the upper tier. How many of us have heard ourselves or a colleague say with a kind of gallows humor, "I'm here to protect my staff!" It's important to remember that our power is limited. It's not that being a good boss doesn't matter. Libraries benefit from managers at every level who listen well, advocate for their colleagues, and are responsive to staff concerns. But when it comes to the big stuff—who gets paid and how much, whether we're working offsite or on, what budget we'll have this year and how we can spend it—those are usually decided well above your pay grade, even if manager, supervisor, or director is in your title.

If union work is about power—thinking about who has it, what it's doing, and how to build it—then it's important for everyone in the workplace to think about their own. Being a boss but not *the* boss comes with all kinds of power: the power to set agendas, support and promote staff, and make final decisions. But that power is always shaped and constrained by the power your boss and their boss and their boss hold and wield in the workplace. Unionized workers bargain collectively with the person at the very top. That's probably not you. You likely have much more in common with the people who work for you than the person you work for. Keeping this in mind can help you support your colleagues as they organize rather than standing in the way.

Unions Make Workers Lazy

It's hard to innovate with a union—my staff refuses to try new things, we could move forward but we're stuck with bad employees—the union protects them, if it wasn't for the union.... These are the kinds of complaints we hear from managers and even other workers who are in unionized workplaces or who are facing a union drive. One of the significant benefits of a negotiated contract is a set of clear guidelines and processes for firing people. That's what makes a union job different from an at-will position: you can't be fired without due process if you're protected by a union contract. And that's a good thing. In workplaces without these kinds of protections, all power resides with the boss who can hire and fire at will, as long as they are in compliance with state, local, and federal laws. With union protections, workers hold on to some of that power. Union contracts give workers more control over their working conditions, including the terms of separation from their employer.

Chapter 9

People often point to this element of unionized workplaces—that it can be harder to fire people—as evidence that unions produce lazy workers. The implicit argument is that the primary way we have to keep workers motivated, engaged, and interested in the work of the organization is the constant threat that their positions may be eliminated. Does this reflect how you manage your staff? Our guess is probably not. Organizing and motivating people to work together to accomplish shared goals is hard work—ask any union organizer! When we focus on unions as the reason that motivating workers is difficult, we miss an opportunity for shared exploration of ways to make work more meaningful for all of us.

Now We Can't Be Friends

When Emily moved from a position covered by a union contract to a manager position, she was, for the first time, on the opposite side of the table from her former union comrades. "It wasn't comfortable," she said. "I was no longer responsible for working with colleagues to shape our demands for a better workplace. I had to be the voice of administrative decisions I didn't always agree with." When people say it can be lonely at the top, this is partly what they mean. When you're in a management position, your structural position in the organization changes. When we say *structural*, we mean that the structure of the workplace itself shapes the relationships we can have with each other, no matter who we are. In Emily's experience, she was strongly pro-union and expected to be able to continue supporting organizing work happening in her unit. Her political commitments to the union were still there, but her structural position meant that she could no longer participate in those conversations. It wasn't because she didn't want to, but because she couldn't. This is structured antagonism (Dundon et al., 2017). Even when the boss and the worker are good friends, in the moments when their relationship is defined by workplace structures, they will be in opposition to each other.

Too often workers and managers take that antagonism personally. When we sit across from each other negotiating increased wages, workplace safety rules, health insurance, retirement, or policies around paid time off and vacation, labor and management have different priorities. Workers seek to maximize pay and benefits. Sometimes management wants the same thing. Everyone should want libraries where workers make enough money to live, feel supported and safe in their workplaces, and have access to high-quality healthcare! More often, management sends negotiators to the table to keep pay and benefits lower than what workers want, sometimes to help generate a profit for the company (in the cases of auto manufacturers or airlines, for example) or to keep budgets within the parameters of shrinking local, state, and federal budgets. When management and labor sit across the table from each other, they are opposed to each other. When we're bargaining, it's not about our hearts and minds or who we are as individuals. It's about the work structure that puts us in opposition.

This is a good time to remember that being in opposition is not a bad thing. In fact, it's in that opposition that we come to an agreement. The point of collective bargaining is not to get and stay mad at each other. It's the opposite. When we bargain, each side brings a set of demands to the table and, when negotiating works like it should, gets at least something of what they want. And we all get a contract that clearly defines wages and working conditions and that outlines processes for resolving disagreements as they emerge.

It's Harder to Work with Unions Than with Workers One on One

Unions have a reputation for making the life of a manager harder—*we always have to be sure we're following the rules, nobody can work out of title, our hands are tied when it comes to giving merit raises to staff who shine.* You've probably had these thoughts before. We invite you to think instead about all the ways that unions and the collectively bargained contracts that come with them can make life as a manager easier.

First, contracts lay out the terms of employment for everyone. Want to know whether your staff can work after hours and for how long? What will the pay rate be for a new hire? No need to guess, ferret out the right person in human resources or the city manager's office to ask, or make it up as you go along. Those terms have been agreed to by everyone at the time the contract was signed. Library workers know that standards make work easier to manage—we invented classification and cataloging systems to do just that for our collections. With a negotiated contract, everyone knows where to look to find definitive answers to questions in the workplace.

Second, a union contract sets the terms of employment until the next time we sit down at the bargaining table together. Want more money, cheaper healthcare, extra vacation time, or a parking pass? Instead of negotiating with each worker individually as these concerns come up, the bargaining process settles the terms all at once and at a time everyone has mutually agreed upon.

Chapter 9

You might be thinking, *That makes sense for a large library system, but I only have twenty employees and I can deal with each individually.* Yes, you probably can, but should you? When we negotiate salaries person by person, we can often end up paying people very differently depending on when they were hired, what our budget was like at the time, and who was in charge when the employee came on board. That can breed resentment and confusion once employees start talking to each other (which they always do!). We also know that what people get paid in the workplace has a lot to do with gender and race. Recent data tell us that women are paid, on average, 22 percent less than men (Gould & deCourcy, 2023), while Black workers are paid 24 percent less than white workers (Wilson & Darity Jr, 2022). And these inequities compound: Black women are paid only 70 percent what white men make. When individuals are left to negotiate on their own, the terms of employment will reflect the deep inequalities that structure American wages. With a union contract, pay is set by job type or classification, not by the person working a particular job. When staff are paid according to salary steps or bands that are collectively rather than individually bargained, it's more likely that everybody will be paid according to their job, not their gender or race. That means a more equitable workplace that enables us to focus on what we're all here to do: provide high-quality library resources and services to the people in our community.

Now That I Know What's Good About a Union, What's Next?

In case after case, unions make a real difference in the lives of American workers. Union workers make higher wages, get better benefits, and have more control over their work than people working without collective bargaining rights. There's a reason people are excited about the union difference! These advantages come at a cost to things like bottom-line profits, and they require management to cooperate and negotiate with workers in ways that recognize worker power. That power is both what the law grants union workers and what individuals build together as they work toward shared demands for themselves and each other in the workplace. It can be exciting to think and act in new ways with organized staff, but you may feel trepidation too. In this section we'll offer strategies for implementing a just workplace once a union is in place.

Keep Talking

Unions structure negotiations around wages and working conditions. Rather than figuring out benefits like salaries and vacation worker by worker, one by one, these issues are considered periodically when the contract is up for review. But that doesn't mean it's the only time management and workers should talk to each other. It's still important—maybe even more important—to maintain open and responsive communication with unionized library workers. Even though years elapse between conversations at the table, the toughest negotiations happen when people are surprised when they get there. Making sure you're in regular conversation with coworkers ensures that you're aware of what they'll be asking for and can advocate for the same demands or be prepared with options that respond to what workers need. Remember, you likely have more in common with the people in the union than not, and advocating for them can mean advocating for yourself. In many workplaces, management enjoys health and retirement benefits that match what's won at the table. Making sure you know what people want helps you too.

Most often, you won't be the person at the actual table—that would be the boss-boss. But you will likely be in the conversation, so it can be useful to have information to share with those who will be at the table. Wages and working conditions will be determined during negotiations at the end of a contract, but you'll want to know what the bargaining unit sees as a priority before you get there. The best way to do that is to keep talking throughout the contract so you can solve problems before they turn into grievances and arrive at the table with solutions closer to what workers want—the farther apart you are, the tougher the talks. In addition to regular supervisory meetings, make time to meet with your union steward to talk about union issues.

Find Your Comrades

If you're new to managing in a union environment, you are not alone! As we've already mentioned, union density has been falling since the Taft-Hartley Act, helped along by labor laws that strongly favor employers. In 2018 the Supreme Court ruled in favor of the plaintiff in the *Janus v. AFSCME* case, further undercutting unions. (The ruling eliminated the agency fee for public sector unions, essentially making the entire country a right-to-work state.) As you learn to manage in a unionized environment, having friends will help. Reach out to library managers who have long worked in unionized environments. These include public, school, and academic libraries in "union towns" like New York City and Chicago as well as newly organized shops in towns across the country like Corvallis, Oregon; East Lansing, Michigan; and Skokie, Illinois. Acknowledging your own trepidation and anxiety is important—any new structure in a workplace can be scary! Talking with people who have managed union shops can keep things in perspective. And one of the easiest ways to find comrades is to speak up—you never know who might be listening.

References

Acadia, S., & Vogt, K. (2023). An introduction to dysfunction in the library workforce. In S. Acadia (Ed.), *Libraries as dysfunctional organizations and workplaces* (pp. 1–51). Routledge. 10.4324/9781003159155-1

American Library Association Committee on Professional Ethics. (2021). *Code of ethics*. www.ala.org/tools/ethics

Applegate, R. (2009). Who benefits? Unionization and academic libraries and librarians. *The Library Quarterly: Information, Community, Policy, 79*(4), 443–463. www.jstor.org/stable/10.1086/605383

Berelson, B. (1939). Library unionization. *The Library Quarterly: Information, Community, Policy, 9*(4), 477–510. www.jstor.org/stable/4302641

Bidgood, J. (2018, March 6). West Virginia raises teachers' pay to end statewide strike. *The New York Times*. www.nytimes.com/2018/03/06/us/west-virginia-teachers-strike-deal.html

Bradbury, A., Brenner, M., & Slaughter, J. (2016). *Secrets of a successful organizer*. Labor Notes.

Cancio, K. (2023, February 24). *Staff union rejects latest counter proposal from Daniel Boone Regional Library* [Press release]. Danie Boone Regional Library Workers United. https://afscmeatwork.org/system/files/dbrlwu_contract_press_release_final.pdf

Davis Kendrick, K. (2021). The public librarian low-morale experience: A qualitative study. *Partnership: The Canadian Journal of Library and Information Practice and Research, 15*(2), 1–32. https://doi.org/10.21083/partnership.v15i2.5932

Davis Kendrick, K., & Damasco, I. T. (2019). Low morale in ethnic and racial minority academic librarians: An experiential study. *Library Trends, 68*(2), 174–212. https://doi.org/10.1353/lib.2019.0036

References

Dean, M. M. (2020, June 26). Black employees at the Free Library are throwing the book at management over racism, safety, and pay equity. *The Philadelphia Inquirer.* www.inquirer.com/news/free-library-philadelphia-racism-black-employees-siobhan-reardon-coronavirus-20200626.html

Dundon, T., Cullinane, N., & Wilkinson, A. (2017). *A very short, fairly interesting and reasonably cheap book about employment relations.* Sage.

Eshelman, W. (1972). Library unionization fronts. *Wilson Library Bulletin, 47,* 132–134.

Ettarh, F. (2018, January 10). Vocational awe and librarianship: The lies we tell ourselves. *In the Library with the Lead Pipe.* www.inthelibrarywiththeleadpipe.org/2018/vocational-awe/

Executive Office of Governor Whitmer. (2023, July 26). *Whitmer signs legislation to recruit and retain educators* [Press release]. www.michigan.gov/whitmer/news/press-releases/2023/07/26/whitmer-signs-legislation-to-recruit-and-retain-educators

Fernandez, A. (2023, December 20). *Daniel Boone Library workers ratify first ever contract for library employees in Missouri* [Press release]. Daniel Boone Regional Library Workers United. https://afscmeatwork.org/system/files/dbrlwu_ratification_press_release_final.pdf

Ferndale Area District Library Workers Union. (2022). *Ferndale Library workers file petition with MERC* [Press release].

Fitzgerald, R. (2020, June 25). Regents approve framework for union recognition. *The University Record.* https://record.umich.edu/articles/regents-approve-framework-for-union-recognition/

Glass, A. (2024, June 20). Project 2025 would undo the NLRB's progress on protecting workers' right to organize. *Center for American Progress.* www.americanprogress.org/article/project-2025-would-undo-the-nlrbs-progress-on-protecting-workers-right-to-organize/

Gould, E., & deCourcy, K. (2023, March 29). Gender wage gap widens even as low-wage workers see strong gains. *Working Economics Blog.* www.epi.org/blog/gender-wage-gap-widens-even-as-low-wage-workers-see-strong-gains-women-are-paid-roughly-22-less-than-men-on-average/

Guyton, T. L. (1975). *Unionization: The viewpoint of librarians.* American Library Association.

Harden, B. T. (2020, July 7). More authors cancel Philadelphia Free Library events to back Black workers. *The Philadelphia Inquirer*. www.inquirer.com/arts/free-library-philadelphia-black-authors-cancel-20200707.html

Higbee, J. (1982). Professional goals and union representation. *Social Responsibilities Roundtable Newsletter, 63*, 5. www.ala.org/rt/sites/ala.org.rt/files/content/SRRT/Newsletters/srrt063.pdf

Hirsch, B. T., Macpherson, D. A., & Even, W. E. (2024). *Union membership, coverage, density and employment by occupation: 2023*. UnionStats. www.unionstats.com/

HoCo Library Workers United. (2023). *We're forming a union!*. https://hclwunited.org/

Iafolla, R., & Purifoy, P. (2023, June 2). Starbucks is racking up labor law violations as rulings roll in. *Bloomberg Law*. https://news.bloomberglaw.com/daily-labor-report/starbucks-is-racking-up-labor-law-violations-as-rulings-roll-in

Johnson, S. (2021, February 11). *A decade after Act 10, it's a different world for Wisconsin unions* [Radio broadcast]. Wisconsin Public Radio. www.wpr.org/economy/labor/decade-after-act-10-its-different-world-wisconsin-unions

McAlevey, J. (2016). *No shortcuts: Organizing for power in the new Gilded Age*. Oxford University Press.

McAlevey, J., & Lawlor, A. (2021). *Turning the tables: Participation and power in negotiations*. UC Berkeley Labor Center.

McAlevey, J., & Lawlor, A. (2023). *Rules to win by: Power and participation in union negotiations*. Oxford University Press.

Mikula, D. E. (2020, April 30). *Curbside service and reopening plans for Michigan libraries*. Michigan Library Association. www.milibraries.org/index.php?option=com_content&view=article&id=821%3Acurbside-service-and-reopening-plans-for-michigan-libraries

Milam, C. H. (1937). Administrative reports. *Bulletin of the American Library Association, 31*(9), 485–544. www.jstor.org/stable/25689176

Milden, J. W. (1977). Women, public libraries, and library unions: The formative years. *The Journal of Library History (1974–1987), 12*(2), 150–158. www.jstor.org/stable/25540731

Murch, D. (2022). *Assata taught me: State violence, racial capitalism, and the movement for Black lives*. Haymarket Books.

References

National Labor Relations Board Office of Public Affairs. (2023, April 5). NLRB region 1—Boston obtains settlement with Chipotle with $240,000 in back-pay and front pay, preferential hiring, and notice posting in 40 stores. *NLRB News & Publications.* www.nlrb.gov/news-outreach/region-01-boston/nlrb-region-1-boston-obtains-settlement-with-chipotle-with-240000-in

Nichols, J. (2024, February 16). Michigan just became the first state in 6 decades to scrap an infamous anti-union law. *The Nation.* www.thenation.com/article/politics/michigan-right-to-work-law

Nourse, L. M. (1934). Staff associations—a job for junior members. *Bulletin of the American Library Association, 28*(12), 873–875. www.jstor.org/stable/25688320

Ohio Federation of Teachers. (2021, October 20). *Workers at Worthington libraries win union vote overwhelmingly* [Press release]. www.oft-aft.org/press/workers-worthington-libraries-win-union-vote-overwhelmingly

Parker, M., & Gruelle, M. (1999). *Democracy is power: Rebuilding unions from the bottom up.* Labor Education and Research Project.

Peet, L. (2017, August 1). Westland PL resets staff, leadership. *Library Journal.* www.libraryjournal.com/story/westland-pl-resets-staff-leadership

Peet, L. (2020, July 24). Free Library of Philadelphia director Siobhan Reardon resigns after criticisms of system-wide racism. *Library Journal.* www.libraryjournal.com/story/free-library-of-philadelphia-director-siobhan-reardon-resigns-after-criticisms-of-system-wide-racism

Phillips, M., Eifler, D., & Page, T. L. (2019). Democratizing the union at UC Berkeley: Lecturers and librarians in solidarity. *Library Trends, 68*(2), 343–367.

Prosten, D. (2020). *The union steward's complete guide* (3rd ed.). David Prosten Books.

Requena, R. (2023, November 22). Niles library board approves first union contract for staff. *Chicago Tribune.* www.chicagotribune.com/2023/11/22/niles-library-board-approves-first-union-contract-for-staff/

Reyes, J. (2021, January 3). Worker strength—labor unions and individuals showed in 2020 that the struggle in the city continues. *The Philadelphia Inquirer.* www.inquirer.com/jobs/labor/labor-unions-workers-covid-philadelphia-2020-20210103.html

Saad, L. (2023, August 30). More in U.S. see unions strengthening and want it that way. *Gallup.* https://news.gallup.com/poll/510281/unions-strengthening.aspx

Schaub, M. (2020, July 8). Whitehead, others cancel Philly library events. *Kirkus Reviews.* www.kirkusreviews.com/news-and-features/articles/whitehead-others-cancel-philly-library-events/

Sneiderman, M., & Lerner, S. (2023). Making hope and history rhyme: A new worker movement from the shell of the old. *New Labor Forum, 32*(1), 70–79. https://doi.org/10.1177/10957960221144966

Tameez, H. (2020, June 4). *The Philadelphia Inquirer's journalists of color are taking a "sick and tired day" after "Buildings matter, too" headline.* NiemanLab. www.niemanlab.org/2020/06/the-philadelphia-inquirers-journalists-of-color-are-taking-a-sick-and-tired-day-after-buildings-matter-too-headline/

University of California Berkeley Labor Relations. (2023). *Contracts (bargaining units).* https://hr.berkeley.edu/labor/contracts

US Bureau of Labor Statistics. (2024, January 23). Union membership rate fell by 0.2 percentage point to 10.1 percent in 2022. www.bls.gov/opub/ted/2023/union-membership-rate-fell-by-0-2-percentage-point-to-10-1-percent-in-2022.htm

Wilson, V., & Darity Jr., W. (2022). *Understanding Black-white disparities in labor market outcomes requires models that account for persistent discrimination and unequal bargaining power.* Unequal Power Project, Economic Policy Institute. https://epi.org/215219

About the Authors

ANGELO MORENO is an organizer for AFSCME Council 31 in Chicago, Illinois. He started his career in libraries in the summer of 2012 as a page at his childhood library. In 2020 he and his coworkers organized a union at the East Lansing Public Library in Michigan and successfully won wage increases and increased job protections for predominantly part-time, low-wage, precarious staff. He has served as a union chair and a bargaining committee member.

KELLY McELROY has worked in public and academic libraries since she was in high school. She is currently an outreach librarian and associate professor at Oregon State University (OSU), where she also helped organize the faculty union, United Academics OSU. As a unionist, she has served on the bargaining team for multiple rounds of bargaining, including as lead negotiator and executive vice president.

MEREDITH KAHN began working in libraries as a first-year college student, and today they are a librarian at the University of Michigan and an elected leader in a union of librarians, archivists, and curators. They were a founding member of their union's organizing committee and a member of the bargaining team for their union's first contract.

EMILY DRABINSKI is an associate professor in the Graduate School of Library and Information Studies at Queens College. She served in multiple union roles including as a member of the executive committee, secretary, and president of the Long Island University Faculty Federation. In 2016, she was locked out by her employer in the first lockout in the history of US higher education. Drabinski was president of the American Library Association in 2023–2024.

Index

A

Abruzzo, Jennifer, 97
acronyms, use of, xvii
Act 10, 43
affiliates, finding, 29–30
agency fees, 12, 105. *See also* dues
agency shops, 12
agitating, 14
American Federation of Teachers (AFT), 39, 46, 52–54
American Library Association (ALA), 4
anti-union legislation, 24, 43. *See also* right-to-work laws
arbitration, 3, 63, 91
Association of American University Professors (AAUP), 39
at-will employees, 2–3

B

backchanneling, 85–86
Baltimore County Public Library (BCPL), 44
bargaining
    basics of, 64–67
    closed, 65
    collective, 63
    committees for, 69–70
    for common good, 73
    in good faith, 64
    impact, 79
    interest-based, 64–65
    mandatory subjects of, 73
    open, 53–54, 65–66
    oppositional, 64, 74–75
    permissive subjects of, 73
    platform for, 70–74
    preparing for, 67
    regressive, 64
    strategies for, 74–78
    team for, 67–70
    timelines related to, 67
    updates on, 77
    wrapping up, 78–79
    See also collective bargaining agreements (CBAs); contracts
bargaining units, 2, 29, 32, 40–42
Berkeley Public Library, 5
Biden, Joe, 97
BIPOC caucus, 53
Boston Public Library (BPL), 47
boycotts, economic, 11
brainstorming, 75
brown, adrienne maree, 14, 55, 56
bullying, 92
Burley, Laurel, 5
bylaws, 34, 35, 36, 68, 69

C

campaigns, 51–62
card checks, 31–32
caucuses, 75, 78
Chipotle United, 24
classifications, differences in, 40–42
closed bargaining, 65
closed shops, prohibitions on, 12
Code of Ethics, ALA's, 5–6
collective bargaining, 63. *See also* bargaining

collective bargaining agreements (CBAs)
   description of, 2
   limitations on, 8
   public-sector employees and, 43
common good, bargaining for, 73
communication with management, 85–87, 105
community support, 45
Concerned Black Workers of the Free Library of Philadelphia, 54–57, 60, 61
conflict, 84–85, 100
constitutions, 34, 35, 36, 68, 69
contract action teams (CATs), 70, 78
contract language, 74, 76
contracts
   bargaining for, 63–81
   benefits of, 103–104
   description of, 2
   discipline and dismissal and, 2–3
   enforcement of, 88–91
   ratifying, 79
   See also bargaining
COVID-19 pandemic, xiii, xiv, xv, 6, 48, 55, 59–60, 79
coworkers, talking to, 13–16, 18, 22–23

D

demand to bargain, 67
disciplinary actions, 3, 36–37
division, attempts at, 19–20
dues
   hesitation regarding, 22
   per caps and, 30
   state laws regarding, 43
   union governance and, 36
   See also agency fees
Dysfunctional Library, The (Henry, Eshleman, and Moniz), 7

E

East Lansing (Michigan) Public Library, 42
economic boycotts, 11
economic proposals, 77
educating, 14, 22
elected officials/politics, 45–49, 97
elections, 31–33, 71
Emergent Strategy (brown), 14, 55

employers/management
   advice for, 99–106
   dealing with, 83–94
   opposition from, 19–20, 32
   rights regarding, 18
   union representatives and, 36–37
equitable treatment, 3
equity, diversity, and inclusion, 72
escalation curves, 61, 70
Eshleman, Joe, 7
Ettarh, Fobazi, 20
executive committees, 34–35
exit strategies, 77

F

fair share fees, 43
fear, 17, 21, 92–93
financial proposals, 77
focus groups, 71
Free Library of Philadelphia, 54–57, 60
fun elements, importance of, 61–62

G

gender inequity, 104
governance, 33–36
grievances, 3, 89–91
ground rules, 66–67
Gruelle, M., 35

H

Henry, Jo, 7
Howard County (Maryland) Library System, 8
human resources (HR), 87

I

impact bargain, 79
impasse, declaring, 67
"in good faith," meaning of, 64
indigenization, 72
individualism, 21
inoculation, importance of, 16–17, 45, 58
interest-based bargaining (IBB), 64–65
internationals, 30
intimidation, 92–93

J

Janus v. AFSCME, 12, 43, 99, 105
just cause, 3

L

Labor Notes, 53
labor-management meetings (LMMs), 87–88, 93
Lawlor, Abby, xii, 66
lazy workers, myth of, 101–102
lead negotiators, 69
leaders, natural, 28
leadership councils, 34–35
Lerner, Stephen, xii
Levinson, Cate, 8
Libraries as Dysfunctional Organizations and Workplaces, 7
Library Journal, 58
listening
 agitation and, 14
 to coworkers, 13–14
 negotiations and, 76
locals, 29

M

management. *See* employers/management
mandatory subjects of bargaining, 73
McAlevey, Jane, xii, 53, 66
membership meetings, 71
middle managers, 100–101
Milam, Carl H., 4
Moniz, Richard, 7
Murch, Donna, xii–xiii

N

National Labor Relations Act (NLRA), 11, 42, 44, 92
National Labor Relations Board, 97
New York Public Library, 3
Niles-Maine District Library, 8
note taking, 76, 86, 87–88

O

officer positions, 34–35
one-on-one conversations, 70
open bargaining, 53–54, 65–66
oppositional bargaining, 64, 74–75
organizer model, 33
organizing committees, forming, 27–29
organizing conversations, 14–16, 21–23

P

packaging, 76–77
pandemic, xiii, xiv, xv, 6, 48, 55, 59–60, 79
Parker, M., 35
per caps, 30
permissive subjects of bargaining, 73
Philadelphia Inquirer, 56, 57
political action funds, 46
political campaigns, contributions to, 11
politics, 45–49, 97
progressive discipline, 3
Public Employee Collective Bargaining Act (PECBA), 67
Public Service Loan Forgiveness program, 46
public-sector employees, 42–45

R

racial justice issues, 53, 54–57, 60, 71–73, 97, 104
rank-and-file members
 democratization and, 52–54, 60
 organizer model and, 33
ratification, 79
recognition, 31–32
relationships, building, 14, 49, 84–85
remote work agreements, 21–22
reporting structures, 41
retaliation, 92–93
rights, knowing, 17–18, 23–24
right-to-work laws, 12, 23, 24, 43
Rosa-Luxemburg-Stiftung Foundation, 53

S

Seattle Central College, 52–54, 60, 61
self-censorship, 17
sidebars, 76
Sneiderman, Marilyn, xii
social justice, 71–72
solidarity, 21, 49, 56, 57, 97
solidarity strikes, 11
staff associations, 4–5
staffing for unions, 35–36

Starbucks Workers United, 24
stewards, 34, 70
Strike School, 53
strikes
    history of, 5
    prohibition of, 43–44, 97
    public-sector employees and, 43–44
    recognition and, 31
    solidarity, 11
    threat of, 96–97
    wildcat, 11
structure tests, 16, 32
structured antagonism, 2, 84, 100, 102
supervisors, 100–101
Supreme Court
    Janus v. AFSCME and, 12, 43, 99, 105
    Weingarten rights and, 36–37
surveys, 70

T

Taft-Hartley Act (1947), 11–12, 99, 105
Taylor Act (1967), 97
team managers, 69
theme-based committees, 71
third-party assertions, 19, 22
Thompson River University Faculty Association, 72
transparency, 52–54, 65, 79
Truman, Harry S., 11
trust, 14

U

unfair labor practices (ULP) charges, 24, 64, 93
union locals, 29
unions
    campaigns for, 51–62
    community support for, 45
    decline in membership in, xvi
    definition of, 2
    democratizing, 52–54
    future of, 95–98
    goals of, xii
    history of, 3–5
    library-specific issues for, 39–50
    membership rates of, 12, 95–96, 105
    motivations for joining, 6–7
    myths about, 100–104
    need for, 6–7
    opposition to, 32
    recognition of, 31–32
    restrictions placed on, 11–12, 23
    retaliation related to, 58
    role of, 1–10
    staff and, 35–36
    starting, 11–25
    structure of, 29–30, 33–36
    support for, 12
    wall-to-wall, 41
    winning, 27–38
United Faculty of Florida, 8
United Federation of Teachers (UFT), 42
University Federation of Librarians, 5
University of California (UC) Berkeley, 5, 42
University of North Florida, 8
US Bureau of Labor Statistics, 95

V

vocational awe, 20
voluntary recognition, 31–32

W

wall-to-wall unions, 41
Weingarten rights, 36–37
Whitehead, Colson, 57
Whitmer, Gretchen, 59
wildcat strikes, 11
wins, celebrating, 96
worker power, building, 13